**New Directions for
Institutional Research**

John F. Ryan
EDITOR-IN-CHIEF

Gloria Crisp
ASSOCIATE EDITOR

Methodological Advances and Issues in Studying College Impact

Nicholas A. Bowman
Serge Herzog
EDITORS

Number 161
Jossey-Bass
San Francisco

𝓗

METHODOLOGICAL ADVANCES AND ISSUES IN STUDYING COLLEGE IMPACT
Nicholas A. Bowman, Serge Herzog (eds.)
New Directions for Institutional Research, no. 161
John F. Ryan, Editor-in-Chief
Gloria Crisp, Associate Editor

NEW DIRECTIONS FOR INSTITUTIONAL RESEARCH (ISSN 0271-0579, electronic ISSN 1536-075X) is part of The Jossey-Bass Higher and Adult Education Series and is published quarterly by Wiley Subscription Services, Inc., A Wiley Company, at Jossey-Bass, One Montgomery Street, Suite 1200, San Francisco, California 94104-4594 (publication number USPS 098-830). POSTMASTER: Send address changes to New Directions for Institutional Research, Jossey-Bass, One Montgomery Street, Suite 1200, San Francisco, California 94104-4594.

INDIVIDUAL SUBSCRIPTION RATE (in USD): $89 per year US/Can/Mex, $113 rest of world; institutional subscription rate: $341 US, $381 Can/Mex, $415 rest of world. Single copy rate: $29. Electronic only–all regions: $89 individual, $341 institutional; Print & Electronic–US: $98 individual, $410 institutional; Print & Electronic–Canada/Mexico: $98 individual, $450 institutional; Print & Electronic–Rest of World: $122 individual, $484 institutional.

EDITORIAL CORRESPONDENCE should be sent to John F. Ryan at jfryan@uvm.edu.

New Directions for Institutional Research is indexed in *Academic Search* (EBSCO), *Academic Search Elite* (EBSCO), *Academic Search Premier* (EBSCO), *CIJE: Current Index to Journals in Education* (ERIC), *Contents Pages in Education* (T&F), *EBSCO Professional Development Collection* (EBSCO), *Educational Research Abstracts Online* (T&F), *ERIC Database* (Education Resources Information Center), *Higher Education Abstracts* (Claremont Graduate University), *Multicultural Education Abstracts* (T&F), *Sociology of Education Abstracts* (T&F).

Cover design: Wiley
Cover Images: © Lava 4 images | Shutterstock

Microfilm copies of issues and chapters are available in 16mm and 35mm, as well as microfi che in 105mm, through University Microfilms, Inc., 300 North Zeeb Road, Ann Arbor, Michigan 48106-1346.

www.josseybass.com

THE ASSOCIATION FOR INSTITUTIONAL RESEARCH (AIR) is the world's largest professional association for institutional researchers. The organization provides educational resources, best practices, and professional development opportunities for more than 4,000 members. Its primary purpose is to support members in the process of collecting, analyzing, and converting data into information that supports decision making in higher education.

Contents

EDITORS' NOTES

Many constituents within and outside of higher education have demanded stronger evidence regarding the extent to which curricular and cocurricular practices promote student learning, achievement, and persistence. Some important statistical and conceptual advances have been made in recent years, but these are only starting to gain attention in higher education and institutional research. This volume is designed to provide resources and information to improve the quality of work examining the impact of college on students. The seven chapters are organized into two parts. The first part provides overviews of three methodological approaches to establish stronger causal inferences with observational data and to improve measurement of student engagement and outcomes; the second section includes four empirical studies on the design and analyses of effective student assessments.

The first two chapters introduce two analytical frameworks suitable for institutional research (IR) practitioners who work with nonrandomized, observational data. Chapter 1 focuses on the regression discontinuity (RD) design and offers an example of how RD can be used to minimize selection bias associated with measuring the effect of financial aid on student outcomes. Chapter 2 extends the discussion on coping with selection bias with an overview of propensity score (PS) analysis and an application of the PS when gauging the impact of campus academic support services. Chapter 3 offers an introduction to Item Response Theory (IRT), which enables IR professionals to measure student traits and activities that are independent of the survey instrument used to collect such data. The value of IRT is illustrated with an example of how to develop and assess a scale measuring student–faculty interaction.

The second part centers on survey methodology and outcomes assessment issues that are integral to gathering valid student data. Chapter 4 examines the meaning and interpretation of college student self-reported gains (which constitute an alternative form of outcomes assessment) and investigates whether these might simply serve as a subset of college satisfaction. Chapter 5 compares and contrasts two approaches for identifying unmotivated test takers who are completing a low-stakes examination (whose data should be removed to obtain meaningful results). The final two chapters discuss practical aspects of questionnaire design in experimental studies. Chapter 6 explores whether the number of online survey pages and the inclusion of a progress bar affect item nonresponse, whereas Chapter 7 examines the impact of item order and item response options on students' overall

NEW DIRECTIONS FOR INSTITUTIONAL RESEARCH, no. 161 © 2014 Wiley Periodicals, Inc.
Published online in Wiley Online Library (wileyonlinelibrary.com) • DOI: 10.1002/ir.20063

responses. Findings from these chapters have important implications for IR practitioners and others who study college impact.

Nicholas A. Bowman
Serge Herzog
Editors

NICHOLAS A. BOWMAN *is an assistant professor of higher education and student affairs at Bowling Green State University.*

SERGE HERZOG *is director of institutional analysis at the University of Nevada, Reno.*

NEW DIRECTIONS FOR INSTITUTIONAL RESEARCH • DOI: 10.1002/ir

1

The goal of this chapter is to provide a brief introduction to one of the most rigorous nonexperimental analytical methods currently employed by education researchers: regression discontinuity.

Applying Regression Discontinuity Design in Institutional Research

Allyson Flaster, Stephen L. DesJardins

Institutional researchers are often tasked with studying the effects of a variety of postsecondary education practices, policies, and processes. Examples include the effectiveness of precollegiate outreach programs such as summer bridge programs; whether first-year experience and developmental classes affect student outcomes; whether students residing in living–learning communities have outcomes that differ from their nonparticipating colleagues; and whether financial aid provision affects student outcomes such as persistence and completion. Given scarce institutional resources and the push for accountability in postsecondary education, decision makers are increasingly interested in whether institutional policies and programs actually achieve their intended goals.

Although a large body of research about the effectiveness of institutional interventions designed to improve student and institutional outcomes exists, there have been calls to improve the rigor of our research (DesJardins & Flaster, 2013; Schneider, Carnoy, Kilpatrick, Schmidt, & Shavelson, 2007). In particular, there has been a push for education researchers to be able to make more rigorous ("causal") claims about our practices, policies, and processes.

Experiments (randomized controlled trials, or RCTs), which are characterized by the random assignment of subjects into treatment and control groups, are considered the "gold standard" for making causal claims (Schneider et al., 2007; Shadish, Cook, & Campbell, 2002). The rationale for conducting experiments is to be able to provide an unbiased estimate of the treatment on an outcome, but RCTs are often impracticable or may even be unethical in some research contexts (see Bielby, House, Flaster, & DesJardins, 2013; DesJardins & Flaster, 2013, for details). There are, however, statistical methods that can be employed when using observational (nonexperimental) data. These quasi-experimental methods attempt to

NEW DIRECTIONS FOR INSTITUTIONAL RESEARCH, no. 161 © 2014 Wiley Periodicals, Inc.
Published online in Wiley Online Library (wileyonlinelibrary.com) • DOI: 10.1002/ir.20064

remedy the inferential problems that arise when units of observation, such as students, are not randomly assigned into treatment or control groups. Even though these methods, some of which are discussed in this volume, do not randomize units into treatment/control status, when properly applied they can substantially reduce any estimation bias due to nonrandom assignment.

Here we provide an introduction to one of these methods: the regression discontinuity (RD) design. In the next section, we discuss a framework often used as the conceptual basis in nonexperimental analyses such as RD.

Overview of the Counterfactual Framework

Many social scientists have employed the *counterfactual framework* in support of analysis designed to make rigorous claims about the effectiveness of institutional practices, policies, or processes ("interventions"). Collectively, these interventions are often referred to as *treatments*. The counterfactual framework posits that, hypothetically, each unit (individuals, classrooms, households, and so on) under study has two potential outcomes: one outcome under treatment and another outcome under nontreatment (Holland, 1986; Murnane & Willett, 2011). Ideally, to determine whether a treatment causes an effect, we would compare each unit's outcome in a world where it received the treatment and then compare its outcome in a counterfactual world where it did not receive the treatment.

For example, imagine we want to determine whether the provision of student financial aid (the treatment) improves the retention rate of students to the sophomore year (the outcome; henceforth, first-year retention). One way to study the effects of the provision of aid on retention is to use the students as controls (counterfactuals) for themselves. We could do this by providing some students with financial aid in their first year of college and then measure whether they are retained to the beginning of the sophomore year. Then, if we had a time machine, we would turn the clock back to the beginning of the freshman year, not give these students financial aid, measure their retention rate at the beginning of year two, and then calculate the difference between the two retention rates. The intuition is that comparing students to themselves under both the treatment and control conditions accounts for all the observed and unobserved factors that may affect their retention to the sophomore year. Thus, any difference in the retention rates between these two groups represents financial aid's *causal effect*, because the treatment condition would be the only factor that was different across these two states of the world. If we did this for a large number of students and averaged over each of their outcomes, we could ascertain an unbiased *average treatment effect* (ATE)—an estimate of the treatment's effect on the population of interest that is purged of influence from (possibly) confounding factors.

NEW DIRECTIONS FOR INSTITUTIONAL RESEARCH • DOI: 10.1002/ir

The fundamental problem in the example provided earlier, and in the application of the counterfactual framework more generally, is that we cannot observe units in these two different states of the world (Holland, 1986). We observe them only under the factual condition (the world we can observe), whereas outcomes under the counterfactual condition remain unknown. This fundamental problem is, essentially, a missing data problem (Murnane & Willett, 2011). For example, assume that the outcome (Y) is retention to the sophomore year and the treatment (T) equals 1 when aid is provided to a student and 0 when it is not. Typically we possess data on the outcome under treatment for those in the treatment group ($Y_1 \mid T = 1$), but not the outcome under treatment for those in the control group ($Y_1 \mid T = 0$), and vice versa.

Researchers often attempt to approximate the counterfactual condition by employing experiments where units are randomized into treatment. When correctly implemented, these designs result in the treated and control groups having (on average) identical observable and unobservable characteristics and differing only with regard to their treatment status (Murnane & Willett, 2011; Schneider et al., 2007). When this is the case, the ATE can be obtained by simply comparing the average outcomes, or the means, for the treated and control groups. When treatment assignment is done using randomization, the mechanism by which assignment takes place is exogenous. In the context of causal inference, *exogeneity* refers to variation that occurs because it is determined outside of the model under analysis and is used to assign units to either the treatment or control condition. Its converse, *endogeneity*, occurs when a unit is assigned to treatment status by an "agent" within the system under study (see Murnane & Willett, 2011, for additional details).

In colleges and universities, endogenous treatment assignment is the norm. Students, a common unit of analysis, often choose the classes they take, the types of financial aid they apply for, and the support services they receive. Similarly, faculty members often choose different types of pedagogy, whether to engage in interdisciplinary research, or whether to participate in technology training. Endogenous treatment assignment complicates making causal inferences about these interventions, because units such as students or faculty who elect to choose a treatment may be systematically different in unobserved or unmeasured ways than those who do not choose treatment. Any unobserved factors that are related to both the receipt of treatment and outcomes are called *confounding* factors. For instance, motivation, which is typically unmeasured in observational data, may affect one's treatment status (whether a student receives aid, which requires an application) and also affect the outcome (e.g., that student's retention). Untangling this confoundedness is a major challenge, one that we can attempt to remedy using different designs and statistical methods.

Randomized trials may be the best method for untangling confoundedness, but it is not always possible to use them to study the effectiveness of a program or policy (Cook, 2002). For example, there may be resistance to randomly assigning students, regardless of their motivation to succeed in their coursework, to participate in a new tutoring program. Furthermore, RCTs necessitate considerable work in the research design stage to ensure that they are properly executed (Murnane & Willett, 2011). This requires institutional researcher involvement with program evaluations *before* treatments are administered. Oftentimes, however, institutional researchers are not asked to evaluate the effectiveness of an intervention until *after* the intervention has been implemented.

Fortunately, over the course of several decades, analytical methods have been developed that can help researchers to make very rigorous inferences when treatment assignment is nonrandom (Cook, Shadish, & Wong, 2008). Of the various analytical approaches used to solve the missing data problem inherent in the counterfactual framework, RD design is generally viewed to be one of the more rigorous nonexperimental methods available for estimating treatment effects (Steiner, Wroblewski, & Cook, 2009; U.S. Department of Education, 2011).

Fundamentals of Regression Discontinuity Design

RD design has a relatively lengthy history within the field of education and program evaluation (Cook, 2008). Thistlethwaite and Campbell employed the technique in the late 1950s to study the effects of "certificates of merit" provided by the National Merit Scholarship (NMS) Program on (a) high school students' ability to obtain funding for college and (b) their plans to pursue advanced degrees. They proposed that legitimate counterfactuals could be produced by capitalizing on a feature of the certificate awarding process: Students were eligible to receive an NMS certificate if they scored at or above a threshold on a standardized test. Thistlethwaite and Campbell (1960) reasoned that—unlike students at opposite ends of the test score distribution—students who narrowly missed earning a certificate (e.g., by one point), and those who received a certificate by scoring at or just above the threshold, shared very similar characteristics. Key to their argument was the assertion that, as is true in a randomized trial, the only substantial observed and unobserved difference between the two groups of students at the threshold margin was that one group was exogenously provided with a treatment by the National Merit Scholarship Corporation and the other was not. Thus, any significant differences in outcomes between the two groups could be attributed to the certificates' treatment effects.

Researchers in education psychology, economics, and statistics have made many contributions to RD's conceptual and practical development since the 1960s (Cook, 2008). We provide an introduction to the method in the following sections, noting when it is appropriate to use RD, some of the assumptions underlying its use, and how to test whether these assumptions are being violated. We do so using a hypothetical example from the world of institutional research. Because this chapter is geared toward researchers who have little to no experience with RD design, we keep detailed technical and conceptual points to a minimum and point interested readers to additional sources where appropriate.

A Hypothetical Example.   Midwest University is a (fictional) large university that is striving to become more socioeconomically diverse. Two years ago, administrators decided to implement a loan replacement grant program for low-income students modeled after similar financial aid programs at Princeton University and the University of North Carolina-Chapel Hill. The grant program, dubbed the "Midwest Compact" (M-Comp), replaces all loans in eligible students' financial aid packages with institutional gift aid that does not need to be repaid. Students are automatically eligible to receive the M-Comp grant if they have a family income lower than a maximum amount set each year by the university. In the first year of the program, only students with a gross family income of $35,000 or less—as reported on their prior year federal income tax form—were eligible to receive the M-Comp grant. In the second year, the income cutoff was increased to $37,000. Approximately 10% of Midwest University undergraduates were eligible to receive the grant each year ($N = 3,050$ in year one; $N = 3,402$ in year two). The family income cutoffs were set by enrollment managers prior to the administration of grant funds, and the specific income cutoffs were not publicly announced prior to students applying for financial aid from Midwest University in either year. The university spent about $5 million on the M-Comp grant program in its first two years of implementation, so administrators were eager to know if the money was well spent. Next we will introduce the basic concepts of the RD design while discussing how an institutional researcher at Midwest University could apply RD to estimate the causal effect of the loan replacement grant program on the first-year retention of recipients.

Running Variable.   A defining feature of RD design is that an individual's probability of receiving the treatment is determined by that person's value on a (typically) continuous variable, referred to as the *running* or *forcing variable* (Imbens & Lemieux, 2008). The point along the running variable at which one's probability of receiving the treatment jumps considerably or discontinuously (hence the name) is called the *cut-point* or *treatment threshold*. In the M-Comp example discussed earlier, the running variable that determines eligibility for treatment is family income, and the cut-points are $35,000 (in year one) and $37,000 (in year two). As a first step in applying RD, the researcher should examine the relationship between the probability of receiving the treatment and the running variable. Figure 1.1 illustrates the case where all students with a value to the left of (or "below") the cut-point (represented by the dashed vertical line at 35) for year one receive the M-Comp grant in their financial aid package, and all students with a value to the right of (or "above") the cut-point do not. In such a case, a student's *probability* of being treated is either 1 or 0,

Figure 1.1. Probability of Receiving M-Comp Grant by Student Family Income in a Sharp Regression Discontinuity Design, Year One

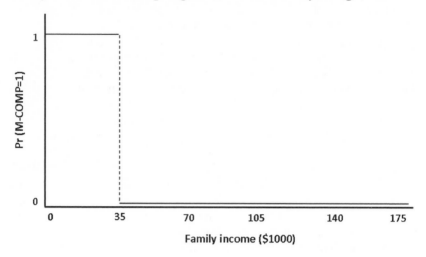

determined wholly by the student's family income. When the probability of treatment is wholly determined by the cut-score, such as in Figure 1.1, the RD design is said to be a "sharp" design (DesJardins, McCall, Ott, & Kim, 2010; McCall & Bielby, 2012). Sharp designs occur when all subjects being studied comply with the threshold-based policy that determines who is in the treatment group and who is in the control group (Lesik, 2008).

However, sometimes there is noncompliance with the mechanism determining treatment assignment. For example, administrators may adjust eligibility criteria, so that individuals who should be placed in the control group based on the established threshold are suddenly eligible for the treatment. In addition, individuals eligible for treatment given the criteria being used to establish the cut-point may opt out of treatment receipt, thereby placing themselves in the control group.

To examine the extent of compliance with the assignment mechanism, an institutional researcher at Midwest University graphed students' probabilities of receiving the M-Comp grant by family income in year one and found that some students whose family income was below the cut-point did not receive the M-Comp grant, and some students whose income was above the cut-point did (see Figure 1.2). After speaking with employees in the financial aid office, the IR staff member learned that the M-Comp grant is a "last dollar" award, meaning that the grant is used to make up the difference between the students' other need- and merit-based scholarships and their total cost of attending Midwest University. Some low-income students received a sufficient amount of federal, state, and departmental scholarships (all of which are applied to need first) to cover their cost of attendance so they did not need the M-Comp grant. The IR staff member also learned

Figure 1.2. Probability of Receiving M-Comp Grant by Student Family Income in a Fuzzy Regression Discontinuity Design, Year One

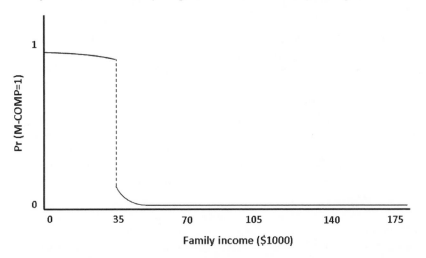

Family income ($1000)

that, occasionally, staff in the financial aid office exercised professional judgment, which is perfectly legitimate, allowing students with family incomes of up to $45,000 to be eligible for M-Comp if they had extenuating circumstances such as a parental job loss within the past year or a family size greater than four.

Earlier we discussed the case when the assignment mechanism is deterministic. In instances where the cut-score does not strictly determine treatment status, but there is a "jump" in the probability of treatment at the cut-score (as in Figure 1.2), the RD is said to be a "fuzzy" design (McCall & Bielby, 2012; Trochim, 1984). In a fuzzy design, treatment assignment is determined by both the exogenous running variable and other factors that are potentially endogenous (DesJardins et al., 2010). This makes the estimation of causal effects a bit more complex. We will discuss the implications of fuzzy designs for making causal inferences in greater detail in the following sections.

Assumptions of Regression Discontinuity. The hypothetical example from the preceding section highlights the importance of understanding the *mechanism(s)* behind treatment assignment when employing RD design. Once the researcher understands the mechanism behind selection into treatment status, and thus whether the RD design for her study will be sharp or fuzzy, she can begin to examine the relationship between the treatment variable and the outcome. First, it is important that researchers have a firm understanding of the assumptions that underlie RD analysis. An important assumption that needs to be checked when using RD is that the observations are randomly distributed near ("locally" around) the cut-point (Lee & Lemieux, 2010). This concept—known as *local randomization*—was fundamental to Thistlethwaite and Campbell's (1960) assertion that, on average, students who barely won and those who just missed winning an NMS certificate were essentially identical in observed and unobserved ways. Perhaps the students who missed earning a certificate by one point were just as meritorious as those just above the threshold, but performed slightly less well on the standardized test that determined treatment because they were, for any number of reasons, having an "off day."

The local randomization assumption holds that if, in a counterfactual world, the National Merit Scholarship Corporation administered the same standardized test to the same group of potential certificate winners again, these students' placement around the test score cut-point would be randomly determined. In other words, students locally distributed around the cut-point when the test was administered the first time would have a 50-50 chance of falling above or below the cut-point the next time the test was administered. *Essentially, the probability of placement into the treatment or control group is akin to a coin-flip for students locally distributed around the cut-point.* These students' treatment group assignment could potentially vary across the two counterfactual worlds only if they do not have perfect control over whether they are treated or not (Lee & Lemieux, 2010). Thus, as discussed previously, another underlying assumption of RD design is that there is some degree of *exogenous variation* in treatment group assignment (Lee & Lemieux, 2010).

Applying local randomization to the M-Comp grant example, an institutional researcher at Midwest University might assume that whether a student's family income is immediately above or below the income cutoff in a given year is determined by random factors, and this assumption can be tested using several methods. One approach is to plot pretreatment characteristics against the running variable (see Imbens & Lemieux, 2008; McCall & Bielby, 2012, for more information). This strategy was used in a study of the effects of the Gates Millennium Scholars (GMS) program on a number of outcomes and explained in detail in McCall and Bielby (2012). To test the assumption of no differences near the cut-point threshold, the researchers regressed the amount of loan aid students received (one of the outcomes of interest) on baseline variables such as the student's gender and SAT score. They then calculated the average predicted values of the outcome for each of the values of the running variable, a noncognitive test score used for treatment assignment. They then plotted the predicted values against the values of the noncognitive test score. This graph allowed them to visually ascertain whether there was a discontinuity in any of the student pretreatment characteristics that corresponds with the running variable (see Figures 5.6 and 5.7 in McCall & Bielby, 2012, for examples of such plots).

Researchers can also check the validity of the local randomization assumption by comparing the average values of pretreatment characteristics immediately around the cut-point (see Calcagno & Long, 2008; DesJardins et al., 2010; Lee, 2008, for more information). For instance, Calcagno and

Long (2008) found that, in their full sample, there were differences in average characteristics such as age and gender between students who were assigned to remedial education (using a standardized test) and those who were not. However, these differences disappeared when only students who scored 10 points above and below the cut-point were compared, implying similarities between the two groups based on (at least) these observable characteristics.

It is also important to examine the running variable's distribution to check for violations of the exogenous treatment assignment assumption (Murnane & Willett, 2011). McCrary (2008) notes that researchers should consider whether individuals in the sample had an opportunity to completely manipulate their values on the running variable. Complete manipulation is likely when individuals (a) know the specific cutoff value prior to treatment assignment, (b) are incentivized to seek the treatment (or not), and (c) have the capacity through time and effort to modify their value on the running variable (see McCrary, 2008, for more information).

For example, suppose Midwest University had announced the income cutoffs for the M-Comp grant in a press release before financial aid applications were due. If students viewed the M-Comp grant as desirable and were able to reduce their work hours so that their family income was just below the maximum to qualify for the grant, then they could perfectly manipulate their treatment status. This would be, however, a violation of the assumption of exogeneity needed to make causal inferences when using the RD method. In such a case, an examination of the data would indicate that more students than expected have family incomes directly below the income cutoff of $35,000, and fewer students than expected have family incomes directly above the cutoff. Luckily, however, administrators at Midwest University did not announce the income cutoffs prior to distributing the grant funds.

Examining the distribution of the treated/nontreated within $100 of each side of the cut-point, an institutional researcher at Midwest University found reassuring visual evidence that students were not manipulating their treatment status (see Figure 1.3). Histograms of family income in years one and two (panels a and b, respectively) do not exhibit large jumps in density

Figure 1.3. Family Income Histograms

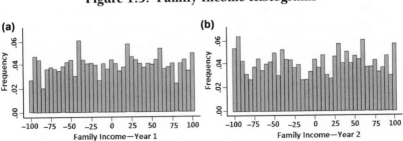

near the M-Comp grant income cutoffs (the points at 0), suggesting that students did not have the ability to completely determine whether they were eligible for the aid. In situations where complete manipulation of treatment status is suspected, researchers may want greater assurance than a simple visual inspection can provide. For examples of a more rigorous test of treatment manipulation when using discrete (noncontinuous) running variables such as family income or standardized tests, see Calcagno and Long (2008) and DesJardins and McCall (2014).

Making Causal Inferences

When they are satisfied that the underlying assumptions discussed earlier cannot be refuted, researchers can begin the process of estimating the causal effect of the treatment on the outcomes of interest. In the case of Midwest University, administrators want to know if the M-Comp grant (the treatment) is effective at inducing students to remain enrolled to their second year (the outcome). The counterfactual conditions they wish to uncover are: (a) what the average retention rate would have been for treated students if these students had not received the grant $(Y_0 \mid T = 1)$ and (b) what the average retention rate would have been for untreated students if these students had received the grant $(Y_1 \mid T = 0)$—outcomes that are impossible to observe without our yet-to-be-invented time machine.

An institutional researcher at Midwest University can construct counterfactuals using data from students immediately around the income cutoff and then project what the retention outcomes would have been for treated students if they had not received the M-Comp grant, and vice versa. The logic behind this approach is illustrated in Figure 1.4, where the average predicted probability of being retained to year two is plotted in an $8,000 window around the cut-point (the point at the double line). For simplicity, the figure depicts a sharp RD design where all students comply with the threshold-based policy. Solid regression lines, which represent the relationship between retention and family income, are fitted to observations on each side of the cut-point. We can use these regression lines to infer what the counterfactual outcomes would have been for students who did and did not receive the grant. When these regression lines cross over the threshold, they become dotted to represent that these portions of the lines are extrapolations into areas where factual data do not really exist.

For example, Figure 1.4 demonstrates that the average predicted probability of retention for students with a family income of $35,000 is approximately 0.80. This is evident by reading the value on the Y axis at the point where the regression line on the left side of the cut-point (the line fitted to the treatment group) crosses the cut-point threshold. If we extrapolate the regression line on the right side of the cutoff (the line fitted to the control group) into the treated group region, its trajectory suggests what the average outcome would have been for treated students if they had not received the

Figure 1.4. Average Probability of Retention by Selected Values of Family Income, Regression Lines Added, Year One

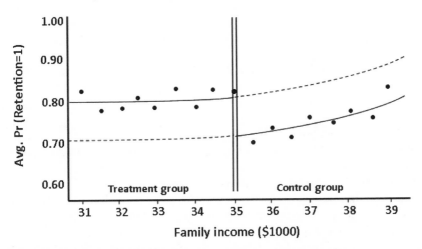

M-Comp grant. The point where this regression line crosses the threshold and intersects the Y axis is 0.72, the counterfactual estimate of the outcome for treated students at the cut-point.

Regression Discontinuity Models.   Figure 1.4 is an illustration of some of the concepts that underlie RD estimation. To formally estimate treatment effects, one needs to model the relationship between the treatment, the running variable, and the outcome among individuals who are locally distributed around the cut-point (Lesik, 2008; Murnane & Willett, 2011). Parametric and nonparametric regression techniques have been used to do just that, but due to space limitations we will only cover parametric techniques in this chapter. However, Imbens and Lemieux (2008) and McCall and Bielby (2012) offer detailed discussions of how to use nonparametric techniques, such as local linear regression, to model the running variable/outcome relationship on each side of the cutoff.

To facilitate interpretation of the treatment effects of the M-Comp grant, we use a linear probability model. Formally, the model could be defined as

$$\Pr(Y = 1) = \beta_0 + \beta_1(M) + \beta_2(X) + \varepsilon, \qquad (1.1)$$

where β_1 represents the effect of the M-Comp grant (M) on the probability of retention ($Y = 1$), β_2 represents the underlying relationship between family income (X) and retention, and ε is a random error term. M is a dichotomous treatment indicator whose value is determined such that $M = 0$ (untreated) if family income (c) $> 35,000$ in year one or $c > 37,000$ in year two, and $M = 1$ (treated) if $c \leq 35,000$ in year one or $c \leq 37,000$ in year two.

Pretreatment variables such as SAT score and demographic variables could also be added to the regression model to decrease variance (improve model power) and test for nonrandomness around the cut-point (McCall & Bielby, 2012). If pretreatment characteristics are significant predictors of the outcome, then individuals in the sample may not be randomly distributed around the cut-point.

For ease of interpretation and to facilitate the combining of data from the two academic years, the institutional researcher at Midwest University could transform ("normalize") the family income running variable to indicate a student's relative distance from the cut-point (using X = family income − cutoff score). Centering the running variable on the cut-score allows one to interpret the intercept as the counterfactual outcome for individuals at the treatment threshold (Murnane & Willett, 2011). Thus, β_0 in Equation 1.1 provides an estimate of what the average probability of retention would have been for students with incomes of \$35,000 (\$37,000) in year one (two) if they had not been eligible for the M-Comp grant.

Choosing a Bandwidth.   One way the RD design differs from traditional regression analysis is that the researcher does not necessarily include the full sample of data in her estimation of the treatment effects. You may recall that Thistlethwaite and Campbell's (1960) intuition for the development of RD was that only students near the test score cut-point were randomly distributed across the certificate of merit threshold. But an important question is: What does "near" the cut-point mean?

One of the goals of RD is to identify a group of individuals assigned to the control group who can serve as reasonable counterfactuals for the treated group. In other words, with the exception of their treatment group assignment, the individuals assigned to be treated are, *on average*, identical to the individuals who are assigned to the control group in all observed and unobserved ways. Of course, it is impossible to know if the average values of unobserved characteristics are the same between the two groups. Nonetheless, researchers need to decide which observations to include in the analysis.

Choosing an analytic window around the cut-point (known as a "bandwidth") often involves striking a balance between the need for power and the need for bias reduction (McCall & Bielby, 2012). Smaller bandwidths reduce the possibility of model misspecification and estimation bias, but can result in imprecise (higher variance) treatment effects estimates if there are too few observations located within the observation window. Although statisticians have not yet identified a minimum sample size needed to conduct valid RD analyses, Bloom (2012) describes a formula to approximate the *minimum detectable effect* (MDE), or "the smallest true treatment effect (or effect size) that has an 80% chance (80% power) of producing an estimated treatment effect that is statistically significant" (p. 64). Researchers can input various sample sizes into this formula to help determine a target MDE. Because RD design requires extrapolation into areas where factual data do not exist, a general rule of thumb is that samples used in RD analyses need to be larger than samples used in randomized trials by a factor of at least 2.72 to produce the same level of precision in their estimates (Bloom, 2012).

After combining the data from year one and year two to (potentially) increase power, the institutional researcher at Midwest University found that there were only 228 students with a family income in a narrow range around the cut-point (arbitrarily defined as + or −$100). Worried that this small sample size would make it difficult to uncover the treatment effect of the M-Comp grant, the IR staff member examined the average values of observable student characteristics in this interval and decided to expand the analytic bandwidth to be $250 on either side of the cutoff. The rationale for increasing the bandwidth was that students assigned to the treatment and control groups within this interval exhibit no statistically significant differences based on their observable characteristics such as sex, race/ethnicity, entering major, and high school GPA. In addition, widening the bandwidth increased the effective sample size to 655 students, more than double the size when the interval around the cut was only $100.

Specifying a Functional Form.   Why is a regression model used in RD, rather than simply approximating a random experiment by taking the difference in the average (mean) outcomes among the treated and untreated students at or near the cut-point? The answer is that it is important to account for the relationship between the running variable and the outcome in order to accurately measure the effect of the treatment on the outcome (Murnane & Willett, 2011). Indeed, many scholars have documented that there is a positive relationship between student family income or social class and college retention (Chen & DesJardins, 2008; Kim, 2007; Walpole, 2003). Most likely, students at Midwest University are no different from students elsewhere in the United States—making those with the greatest access to material resources the most likely to be retained in college. Thus, even if the M-Comp grant had never been implemented, differences in the average probability of retention could have existed between students whose family incomes are just below and above the threshold. By modeling the relationship between the running variable and the outcome, we help ensure that the M-Comp treatment effect (β_1) on Equation 1.1 is purged of underlying relationships such as the income and retention correlation.

However, including the running variable in the analysis requires that the researcher accurately model the functional form of the regression (Lesik, 2008; McCall & Bielby, 2012; Murnane & Willett, 2011). Relationships may not always be linear; for example, family income may have differential impacts on student education outcomes at lower levels than at higher levels of income. Thus, it is important to consider the possibility that the slope of the relationship between the running variable and the outcome may differ on opposite sides of the cut-point and across the values of the running variable.

Researchers can use several methods to attempt to identify the correct functional form between the running variable and the outcome, thereby helping to avoid model misspecification bias (Lesik, 2008). One useful approach is to begin by graphing the relationship between the running variable and the outcome and then fitting a line that appears to best approximate the relationship (Lesik, 2007, 2008; McCall & Bielby, 2012). For example, Lesik (2007) used a nonparametric *lowess smoothing* technique to graph the relationship between a course placement test score and college retention. The graph indicated that, in her sample, a linear logit transformation was appropriate for data on both sides of the cut-point.

Another approach to find the correct functional form is to include higher orders of the running variable—such as quadratic or cubic—or interactions between the running variable and the treatment variable in the regression (Lesik, 2008; Murnane & Willett, 2011). Using this approach, DesJardins and McCall (2014) found that a model with a quadratic form of the noncognitive test score used to assign GMS scholarships was the most appropriate specification.

Although it is advisable to check for the appropriate functional form, in practice it may not be as critical when one is modeling using data very close to the cut-point—especially if there are very large samples in this interval. This is because the smaller the analytic bandwidth, the more likely it is that the slope of the regression line is approximately linear in this smaller interval (McCall & Bielby, 2012).

Estimating Treatment Effects.   In a sharp RD design, the treatment effect is the parameter associated with the dichotomous treatment indicator. This treatment effect is estimated using only data in a window around the cut-point. In Equation 1.1, the parameter β_1 reflects what the ATE of the M-Comp grant would have been for students at the cut-point had all students and staff at Midwest University complied with the threshold-based policy. Therefore, the treatment effect is referred to as the *local average treatment effect* (LATE; McCall & Bielby, 2012). The LATE can be visualized in Figure 1.4 as the vertical distance between the two regression lines evaluated at the cut-point. It is important to note that the LATE is a measurement of the estimated treatment effect for students *at the margin* of receiving the intervention being studied. In our M-Comp grant example, the marginal students are those whose family income places them directly at the cut-point (those with family incomes of $35,000 and $37,000). We can also make the assumption that the LATE reflects the effect of the treatment on those who are included in the analytical bandwidth (for instance, students with a family income of $34,800 in year one). However, as individuals far from the cut-point are often not included in an RD analysis, no inferences should be made as to how the treatment affects their behavior (Murnane & Willett, 2011). Given that the treatment effect (LATE) is local, it may not be an accurate estimate of the M-Comp grant's effect on students from families with very low income levels (e.g., $0 to $5,000).

But as noted earlier in the chapter, the mechanisms underlying the M-Comp grant may not be amenable to a sharp RD design. Some low-income students assigned to the treatment group based on their family income did not actually receive the grant because they had already received the maximum financial aid allowable. Also, some students with incomes above the threshold (those who were assigned to the control group) received the grant (were treated) due to an administrative intervention. Individuals whose assigned treatment group and actual treatment group differ are referred to as *crossovers* (Shadish et al., 2002).

There are several approaches that researchers can use to account for crossovers in an RD design. One approach is to estimate a sharp RD model, such as in Equation 1.1, and redefine the study's research question to be an examination of the effect of being *offered* a treatment rather than the effect of actually having *received* a treatment. This is known as an *intent-to-treat* analysis (Shadish et al., 2002). If the institutional researcher at Midwest University were to take this approach, her analysis would produce an estimate of the effect of having an *income at or below the M-Comp cut-point* on an individual's probability of retention, not an estimate of M-Comp *receipt* on retention.

However, an intent-to-treat analysis does not always answer the substantive questions that educational stakeholders have about the effectiveness of an intervention. For example, the administrators at Midwest University want to know if the M-Comp grant program improved the likelihood of retention for actual recipients, not students who were just income-eligible to receive the grant. Thus, another approach the IR staff member could take is to eliminate crossovers from the sample and estimate Equation 1.1. This approach is only appropriate if crossovers constitute a small proportion of the sample—typically 5% or less—or are confined to a narrow range of the running variable immediately around the cut-point (Shadish et al., 2002; Trochim, 1984). If eliminating crossovers is not an option, then one could use instrumental variable (IV) methods. Space restrictions prevent us from illustrating how to employ IV estimation here, but an example of IV use in educational evaluation can be found in Bielby et al. (2013).

Sensitivity Analysis. A crucial step in conducting an RD analysis is to check the sensitivity of the estimated treatment effects to variations in the model specification. Point estimates that are stable across model specifications provide more believable evidence of the LATE than is the case when such estimates change depending on the regressors included, their form (quadratic, cubic), or the estimation bandwidth chosen. In particular, it is important to check how sensitive the estimates are to changes in the bandwidth and the specification of the functional form of the running variable/outcome relationship. Table 1.1 presents the institutional researcher's (hypothetical) parameter estimates of M-Comp's ATE on recipients' probability of first-year retention, using various bandwidths. Administrators may

**Table 1.1. Parameter Estimates of M-Comp ATE on One-Year
Retention Across Various Bandwidths**

	Cutoff Score ±$250 (Model 1)	Cutoff Score ±$350 (Model 2)	Cutoff Score ±$450 (Model 3)	Cutoff Score ±$550 (Model 4)
ATE	0.079	0.085	0.100	0.111
SE	0.038	0.032	0.028	0.027
N	655	827	1101	1290

be relieved to note that the treatment estimates across all bandwidths suggest a positive effect of the grant on retention to the sophomore year.

Note that Model 1, which has the most restrictive bandwidth, estimates that the M-Comp grant increases recipients' probability of first-year retention by 7.9 percentage points, and this result is significant at conventional levels ($t = 2.08$; $p < .05$). The results from Models 2, 3, and 4, each of which has wider bandwidths, provide estimates that the grant increases retention by a statistically significant 8.5, 10.0, and 11.1 percentile points, respectively.

In addition to checking for robustness across bandwidths, one should test the sensitivity of the results to the functional form of the model. Shadish et al. (2002) recommend overfitting a test case model by including higher order polynomial terms of the running variable (quadratic/cubic terms) and interactions of these with the treatment indicator. Then the analyst successively removes these variables from the regression model and uses fit statistics, such as an F test when using ordinary least-squares regression or likelihood ratio tests when using logistic regression, to test whether the constrained models (the ones with the higher order/interaction terms) are a better fit to the data than the models that do not include these variables (the unconstrained models). (Interested readers should consult Lesik [2008] for more details about this approach, and see pp. 269 and 270 in McCall and Bielby [2012] for an example of how to present and interpret the results of a model that is estimated with linear, quadratic, and cubic terms.)

Conclusion

Institutional researchers have been very successful in informing education decision makers about the factors that are *correlated* with educational outcomes, but we have been less successful in determining whether there are *causal* linkages among interventions and educational outcomes. One reason may be researchers' failure to apply designs and methods that can help unravel the causal effects of educational treatments on outcomes. Given the push for researchers to better understand the causal mechanisms underlying much of what we study, it is incumbent on us to employ the types of methods that will allow us to better understand what programs, policies, and practices are truly effective. Doing so has the potential to improve institutional decision making and, by extension, the prospects of the varied stakeholders we serve. We hope this chapter and the references provided throughout it, along with the other chapters in this volume, will help inform institutional researchers about the utility and proper applications of these methods.

References

Bielby, R. M., House, E., Flaster, A., & DesJardins, S. L. (2013). Instrumental variables: Conceptual issues and an application considering high school course taking. In M. B. Paulsen (Ed.), *Higher education: Handbook of theory and research* (pp. 263–321). Dordrecht, the Netherlands: Springer.

Bloom, H. S. (2012). Modern regression discontinuity analysis. *Journal of Research on Educational Effectiveness*, 5(1), 43–82.

Calcagno, J. C., & Long, B. T. (2008). *The impact of postsecondary remediation using a regression discontinuity approach: Addressing endogenous sorting and noncompliance* (Working Paper No. W14194). Washington, DC: National Bureau of Economic Research.

Chen, R., & DesJardins, S. L. (2008). Exploring the effects of financial aid on the gap in student dropout risks by income level. *Research in Higher Education*, 49(1), 1–18.

Cook, T. D. (2002). Randomized experiments in educational policy research: A critical examination of the reasons the educational evaluation community has offered for not doing them. *Educational Evaluation and Policy Analysis*, 24(3), 175–199.

Cook, T. D. (2008). "Waiting for life to arrive": A history of the regression-discontinuity design in psychology, statistics and economics. *Journal of Econometrics*, 142(2), 636–654.

Cook, T. D., Shadish, W. R., & Wong, V. C. (2008). Three conditions under which experiments and observational studies produce comparable causal estimates: New findings from within-study comparisons. *Journal of Policy Analysis and Management*, 27(4), 724–750.

DesJardins, S. L., & Flaster, A. (2013). Non-experimental designs and causal analyses of college access, persistence, and completion. In L. W. Perna & A. P. Jones (Eds.), *The state of college access and completion* (pp. 190–207). New York, NY: Routledge.

DesJardins, S. L., & McCall, B. P. (2014). The impact of the Gates Millennium Scholars Program on college and post-college related choices of high ability, low-income minority students. *Economics of Education Review*, 38, 124–138.

DesJardins, S. L., McCall, B. P., Ott, M., & Kim, J. (2010). A quasi-experimental investigation of how the Gates Millennium Scholars Program is related to college students' time use and activities. *Educational Evaluation and Policy Analysis*, 32(4), 456–475.

Holland, P. W. (1986). Statistics and causal inference. *Journal of the American Statistical Association*, 81, 945–970.

Imbens, G. W., & Lemieux, T. (2008). Regression discontinuity designs: A guide to practice. *Journal of Econometrics*, 142(2), 615–635.

Kim, D. (2007). The effect of loans on students' degree attainment: Differences by student and institutional characteristics. *Harvard Educational Review*, 77(1), 64–100.

Lee, D. S. (2008). Randomized experiments from non-random selection in US House elections. *Journal of Econometrics*, 142(2), 675–697.

Lee, D. S., & Lemieux, T. (2010). Regression discontinuity designs in economics. *Journal of Economic Literature*, 48(2), 281–355.

Lesik, S. A. (2007). Do developmental mathematics programs have a causal impact on student retention? An application of discrete-time survival and regression-discontinuity analysis. *Research in Higher Education, 48*(5), 583–608.

Lesik, S. A. (2008). Studying the effectiveness of programs and initiatives in higher education using the regression-discontinuity design. In J. Smart (Ed.), *Higher education: Handbook of theory and research* (pp. 277–297). Dordrecht, the Netherlands: Springer.

McCall, B. P., & Bielby, R. M. (2012). Regression discontinuity design: Recent developments and a guide to practice for researchers in higher education. In J. Smart & M. Paulsen (Eds.), *Higher education: Handbook of theory and research* (pp. 249–290). Dordrecht, the Netherlands: Springer.

McCrary, J. (2008). Manipulation of the running variable in the regression discontinuity design: A density test. *Journal of Econometrics, 142*(2), 698–714.

Murnane, R. J., & Willett, J. B. (2011). *Methods matter: Improving causal inference in educational and social science research.* New York, NY: Oxford University Press.

Schneider, B., Carnoy, M., Kilpatrick, J., Schmidt, W. H., & Shavelson, R. J. (2007). *Estimating causal effects using experimental and observational designs.* Washington, DC: American Educational Research Association.

Shadish, W. R., Cook, T. D., & Campbell, D. T. (2002). *Experimental and quasi-experimental designs for generalized causal inference.* Belmont, CA: Wadsworth Cengage Learning.

Steiner, P. M., Wroblewski, A., & Cook, T. D. (2009). Randomized experiments and quasi-experimental designs in educational research. In K. E. Ryan & J. B. Cousins, (Ed.), *The Sage handbook of educational evaluation* (pp. 75–95). Thousand Oaks, CA: Sage.

Thistlethwaite, D. L., & Campbell, D. T. (1960). Regression-discontinuity analysis: An alternative to the ex-post facto experiment. *Journal of Educational Psychology, 51*(6), 309–317.

Trochim, W. M. (1984). *Research design for program evaluation: The regression-discontinuity approach.* Beverly Hills, CA: Sage.

U.S. Department of Education. (2011). *What Works Clearinghouse: Procedures and standards handbook* (version 2.1). Washington, DC: Author. Retrieved from http://ies.ed .gov/ncee/wwc/pdf/reference_resources/wwc_procedures_v2_1_standards_handbook .pdf

Walpole, M. (2003). Socioeconomic status and college: How SES affects college experiences and outcomes. *The Review of Higher Education, 27*(1), 45–73.

ALLYSON FLASTER is a doctoral candidate and research assistant in the Center for the Study of Higher and Postsecondary Education at the University of Michigan.

STEPHEN L. DESJARDINS is professor in the Center for the Study of Higher and Postsecondary Education and professor in the Gerald R. Ford School of Public Policy at the University of Michigan.

2

Estimating the effect of campus math tutoring support, this study demonstrates the use of propensity score weighted and matched-data analysis and examines the correspondence with results from parametric regression analysis.

The Propensity Score Analytical Framework: An Overview and Institutional Research Example

Serge Herzog

Like the previous chapter on the application of regression discontinuity (RD), this study focuses on a quasi-experimental approach, namely propensity score (PS) analysis, for measuring program impact on student success. The importance of moving beyond correlational analysis and estimating causal relationships in education research has been stressed for some time (Angrist, 2003; Morgan & Winship, 2007; Murnane & Willett, 2010; U.S. Department of Education, 2003). Since randomized control trials (RCTs) are costly, raise ethical issues, and are fraught with operational difficulties, they are typically not available to institutional research (IR) practitioners. Instead, institutional research has to rely on techniques that attempt to mimic random assignment in order to reduce selection bias with observational data. Like RD and instrumental variable (IV) design, PS methods offer ways to address selection bias and to establish control groups as benchmarks to gauge treatment effects associated with student participation in educational programs.

Analysis outside institutional research has seen an exponential growth in the application of PS methods since 2000, and the rising number of PS-based higher education studies has prompted scrutiny on its contribution to enhance outcome assessment (Austin, 2008; Bai, 2011; Shadish, 2013; Thoemmes & Kim, 2011). Since PS methods have not been widely used in institutional research, this chapter provides a brief review of the PS concept and previous applications in education research, addresses best practices for PS-based studies, and demonstrates how the PS can be used by institutional research practitioners and scholars to assess the impact of student-selected academic support.

NEW DIRECTIONS FOR INSTITUTIONAL RESEARCH, no. 161 © 2014 Wiley Periodicals, Inc.
Published online in Wiley Online Library (wileyonlinelibrary.com) • DOI: 10.1002/ir.20065

The Propensity Score and Counterfactual Inference Model

Use of the PS in observational studies was popularized by Rosenbaum and Rubin (1983, 1984) and is closely linked to the counterfactual analytical framework that emerged in statistics and econometrics (Heckman, 2000; Holland, 1986; Rosenbaum, 2002; Rubin, 2006). The counterfactual model seeks an answer to the "what if" question. In the context of the example presented here, what is the potential outcome for a student who received academic support had that student not chosen to get support? In other words, a student has potentially two outcomes, but only one can be observed (as discussed in greater detail in the previous chapter). In order to measure this unobserved outcome, one has to account for the likelihood (or predisposition) of a student selecting academic support when measuring the relationship between academic support and the outcome of interest. To render the correlation insignificant between a student's chance to get academic support (i.e., the "treatment") and the outcome of interest (e.g., enrollment persistence), one has to have a comparator case, a student with equal or similar chance to select the treatment but did not, and who can be equally observed like the "treated" student with respect to the outcome. The ability to create a counterfactual case—the comparable untreated student that substitutes for the unobserved outcome of the treated student—is at the core of causal inference estimation after controlling for treatment selection (i.e., selection bias).

Rosenbaum and Rubin (1983) showed that matching a treated case with an untreated case on a single probability (propensity) score that adequately captures the linear combination of factors that predict treatment selection offers a way to reduce selection bias. Formally, the propensity score

$$\hat{p}(X_i) = \Pr(D_i = 1 \mid X_i)$$

measures the probability (Pr) of selecting into treatment D conditional on observable predictors (covariates X) for each case i. Assuming that the treatment can be measured dichotomously ($D = 1$ or 0), the average treatment effect (ATE) conditional on X is formalized as

$$E(\Delta_i \mid X_i = x) = E[(Y_i \mid D_i = 1) - (Y_i \mid D_i = 0)] \mid X_i = x,$$

where $E(\Delta_i \mid X_i = x)$ is the expected difference in the outcome Y_i between the treated ($D_i = 1$) and untreated ($D_i = 0$), controlling for observable factors ($X_i = x$) that predict treatment (D) selection. Since program evaluation in education is focused typically on intervention or support for those students who need it (e.g., math tutoring), the counterfactual centers on the treated—that is, had they not been treated—and thus the average treatment effect on the treated (ATT) is defined as

$$E(\Delta i \mid D_i = 1) = E[(Y_i \mid D_i = 1) - (Y_i \mid D_i = 0)] \mid D_i = 1,$$

New Directions for Institutional Research • DOI: 10.1002/ir

or the difference in outcome under treatment and nontreatment for those who actually experienced the treatment. Since only the treated outcome $(Y_i | D_i = 1)$ is observed for the treated, the untreated outcome $(Y_i | D_i = 0)$ is derived from untreated cases with similar or identical chance of treatment selection as the treated based on observable characteristics (Xs).

The effectiveness of the PS to yield unbiased causal effect estimates hinges on the selection of observables (known as the conditional independence assumption, strongly ignorable treatment assignment, or unconfoundedness) to render treatment selection independent of the potential outcomes for the treated and untreated. That is to say, the likelihood of treatment selection does not affect the outcome of interest. (For example, the chance of receiving math tutoring does not influence the student's math grade.) This independence cannot be established empirically, but must be anchored in covariate selection that is guided by explicit theory and an understanding of the assignment process that leads to treatment selection (e.g., factors that prompt students to seek academic support). Thus, only observable predictors that temporally precede the treatment experience can be used in the PS estimation. The PS must also show sufficient overlap in distribution between treated and untreated cases to produce a comparator case, the individual covariates used in estimating the PS should be closely balanced to rule out bias associated with observable characteristics, and the outcome of interest for a given individual should not be influenced by the treatment status of other individuals (known as the Stable Unit Treatment Value Assumption; see Rubin, 1980). While the first two conditions can be ascertained empirically ex post facto, the last condition is best addressed with a study design that minimizes (or rules out) interaction between treated and untreated, or by capitalizing on natural settings where intergroup mingling is less likely.

After calculating the PS with a logit or probit regression model for a binary treatment (i.e., receiving academic support or not), the treatment effect on the outcome of interest can be estimated by matching treated and untreated cases on the PS, by stratifying cases into subclasses (ranges) of the PS, by inverse probability of treatment weighting (IPTW) using the PS, or by including the PS and treatment indicator in covariate-adjusted regression (Austin, 2011a; Murnane & Willett, 2010). Unlike standard regression that uses parametric specification to account for covariate effects, application of the PS relaxes the linearity assumption through preprocessing of the data either by matching on a single metric to establish a control group (untreated) in order to directly measure the difference in outcome to the treated group (nonparametric), or through preselecting or weighting cases in semiparametric covariate regression.

The heuristic example that follows illustrates each step of the PS method, including PS estimation, application of matching algorithms, checking of common support and covariate balance, and comparison of the estimated treatment effect using different PS methods vis-à-vis

NEW DIRECTIONS FOR INSTITUTIONAL RESEARCH • DOI: 10.1002/ir

parametric regression. The example uses data commonly available to the institutional research practitioner and considers design and measurement issues discussed in previous PS-based studies.

Literature Review

Thoemmes and Kim (2011), Austin (2011a), Stuart (2010), Caliendo and Kopeinig (2008), Morgan and Harding (2006), and Luellen, Shadish, and Clark (2005) offer general introductions to PS methods with observational data, and Reynolds and DesJardins (2010) furnish a detailed example in higher education. PS methods have been used to estimate college selection effects on educational attainment (Brand & Halaby, 2006; Brand & Xie, 2010; Doyle, 2009; Melguizo, Kienzl, & Alfonso, 2011), the impact of campus residency and first-year seminars on retention (Clark & Cundiff, 2011; Schudde, 2011), the influence of course selection on student moral development (Grunwald & Mayhew, 2008), the effect of college major and selectivity on postgraduate outcomes (Black & Smith, 2004; Olitsky, 2014; Titus, 2007), and the relationship between student financial aid and academic success (Herzog, 2008), to name a few areas.

Several issues have emerged from prior studies that inform the design and proper application of PS methods in higher education research. First, the covariates to estimate the probability of treatment selection must be measured, or known, prior to the treatment experience. Variables potentially affected by the treatment should be excluded in the PS estimation, though they may be included as covariates in the outcome model (Stuart, 2010). Covariate selection governed strictly by statistical significance (alpha level) or explained variance (R^2) in the estimation model should be avoided. Instead, preference should be given to sets of variables that maximize covariate balance between treated and untreated, and that are steeped in theory and informed by the treatment selection process.

Not all variables related to treatment and outcome need to be included; only a sufficient number to delink selection into treatment from the outcome is required (Gangl, 2010; Pearl, 2000). Variables not included in the PS estimation are controlled for to the extent that they are correlated with those included in the PS. Therefore, a broad set of covariates will more likely reduce hidden bias due to unmeasured confounders (Bai, 2011; Stuart, 2010). In a review of 86 PS-based studies covering the social sciences (including 34 in the field of education), Thoemmes and Kim (2011) counted an average of 31 (with a median of 16) covariates used in the PS estimation.

However, the number of covariates may be less critical than what types are included in PS estimation. Studies by Steiner, Cook, Shadish, and Clark (2010) and Cook, Steiner, and Pohl (2009) compared the results from a within-study randomized group and self-selected group. They showed that among five types of covariates used in PS estimation to predict mathematics and vocabulary proficiency, proxy pretest measures and student subject

NEW DIRECTIONS FOR INSTITUTIONAL RESEARCH • DOI: 10.1002/ir

preference alone controlled for selection bias. In contrast, student demographic attributes and prior academic achievement variables enhanced bias reduction when added, but they removed little bias by themselves. The fifth construct, student psychological predisposition, was not associated with any bias reduction. Since RCTs are a challenge to conduct, the finding that pretest measures and student proclivity (or motivation) for the subject matter are critical to bias reduction should guide covariate selection for PS estimation.

Shadish (2013) considers results from this within-study comparison as "proof-of-concept" that PS-based analysis may produce results that approximate those from randomized trials (p. 130). The potential for PS analysis to mimic an RCT may also depend on the local and focal similarity between the treatment and control group (e.g., keeping the analysis limited to students from one institution with focus on one specific treatment). Data examined by Steiner et al. (2010) from the within-study comparison groups came from one introductory psychology course at one institution, thus ensuring pretreatment homogeneity in location, time, and measurement process. Though limiting the potential for causal inference to one specific setting, the focal local controls associated with narrow, single-institution studies reduce the number of potential confounds and heighten plausibility of ignorable treatment assignment.

When employing the PS to establish matched treatment and control groups, sample size and density distribution in the PS across each group determine the common support area (i.e., the PS overlap between treated and untreated cases) and the quality of the match. Both are also affected by the choice of the matching algorithm, as illustrated in the heuristic example that follows. Although the principal advantage of PS matching over parametric regression is the exclusion of incomparable cases with little or no PS overlap, testing of the ATT counterfactual should strive to retain all treated cases in the matching process. In small samples with limited common support and few untreated cases, one-on-one matching with replacement may be the best option to reduce bias. Conversely, large samples with a high ratio of untreated to treated cases force a smaller trade-off between bias and variance in the density function (as detailed in Caliendo & Kopeinig, 2008). Shadish (2013) examined the impact of sample size and found that small samples ($n < 500$) are more likely to increase selection bias, while the odds of greater bias is virtually nil with samples of at least 1,500 cases.

In their review of PS-based studies, Thoemmes and Kim (2011) reported that two thirds examined the covariate balance between the matched and weighted groups strictly on the basis of significance tests (t or chi-square statistic). Such tests should be avoided, since they measure balance across samples of varying sizes (depending on the matches or weights) without inference on a broader population; moreover, significant differences in balance may not be detected in smaller samples. Austin (2008, 2011a) and Thoemmes and Kim (2011) recommend the standardized difference in means between treated and untreated groups, which was the chosen metric to compare the quality of covariate balance associated with 15 distinct combinations of PS estimators and matching/weighting algorithms (Harder, Stuart, & Anthony, 2010). The absolute standardized difference in means should be less than 0.25, and closer to zero for covariates that are strongly associated with the outcome of interest (Stuart, 2010). For continuous numeric covariates, density distribution histograms, quantile–quantile plots, and boxplots offer graphical evidence of covariate balance between treated and untreated groups.

When estimating the treatment effect directly from the mean difference in outcome between the matched groups, Austin (2008) reasons that matched cases in each group no longer form two independent samples. Thus, the difference in outcome should be assessed with tests that take into account the paired nature of the data (e.g., dependent t test or McNemar's test for continuous or categorical outcomes, respectively). In contrast, Stuart (2008) explains that the goal of the PS method is to establish similarity between *groups* of individuals on the basis of their PS and balance in the *distribution* of covariates that are captured by the PS. The PS method thus relies on matched groups, not matched pairs of individual cases. The theory for matching on groups has been developed by Rubin and Thomas (1996, 2000). Therefore, the diagnostic tools to evaluate suitability of the PS method—mainly adequate common support and covariate balance—focus on group differences that call for unpaired or independent group tests.

Lastly, Abadie and Imbens (2008) caution that the standard bootstrap, typically used with resampled data, fails to produce asymptotically valid standard errors of the estimated treatment effect when using nearest neighbor matching with replacement (i.e., using the best control case repeatedly). Caliendo and Kopeinig (2008) also address this issue and explain an alternate formula to estimate standard errors introduced by Lechner (1999).

A Heuristic Example: Estimating the Effect of Math Tutoring Support

This section describes the sources of data, measures calculated from the raw data, and the selected PS methods for the analysis before discussing the statistical findings.

Data Source and Measures.   To illustrate the application of the PS in an institutional research context, the following example estimates the impact of the campus math tutoring center on academic success and student enrollment persistence. Data are drawn from a moderately selective university (average SAT of 1080, ACT of 23) and capture the profile and academic experience of new first-year undergraduate students who enrolled in the fall semester of 2011 and 2012 ($n = 4,887$). Academic success is measured with a 100-point momentum index composed equally of first-semester and first-year cumulative grades (GPA) and course credits completed. The use of academic momentum indices to gauge student success goes back to the work of Adelman (2006), and academic momentum of first-year students is highly predictive of degree completion beyond precollege preparation and sociodemographic background (Attewell, Heil, & Reisel, 2012). Enrollment persistence indicates whether or not the student reenrolled for the second semester (fall-to-spring) and for the second year (fall-to-fall).

The treatment group consists of the 780 students who used the math tutoring center at least once in the first semester. The probability of being in that treatment group was estimated for all students on the basis of 25 covariates that capture students' sociodemographic profile (being age 19 or older, male, non-Asian ethnic minority, father has four-year college degree, mother has four-year college degree, out-of-state residency, in-state residency outside of local area, Pell Grant award), academic preparation (high school GPA, ACT/SAT math test score, high school class rank percentile, advanced standing at entry), academic motivation and plan (delayed college entry by six months or more, ACT/SAT test date, institution is first choice, undeclared major, plans to attend graduate school), living and work plans (lives on campus, signed up for a living-and-learning community, plans to work full time, does not plan to work), and financial aid profile (received loan aid, received scholarship aid, has unmet need). Except for the high school GPA and percentile rank, the math test score, and the test date, all covariates are dummy variables (no = 0, yes = 1). The test date is a continuous metric that measures the months elapsed between the first time the student took the ACT/SAT test and the start of the first semester. Advanced standing indicates if a student earned college credit in high school. All data originated with the institution's matriculation system, except for several student self-reported data elements that were recorded as part of the mandatory start-of-semester orientation survey. They include measures of parent level of education, intent to attend graduate school, plans to work full-time or plans to not work while in college (plans to work half-time being the reference category), and having selected the institution as first choice. Use of the math tutoring center was determined from an electronic log that confirmed student use during the first semester (0 = no, 1 = yes).

Selection of the covariates to estimate the PS is governed by several criteria. First, they are all pretreatment baseline characteristics that exist prior to student use of the math tutoring center and thus are not being affected by treatment assignment. Second, all of the covariates may be related to both treatment selection (i.e., using the math tutoring center) and the outcome of interest (i.e., student academic success and enrollment persistence). While the most important covariates are those related to treatment assignment, both theoretical and empirical research show that PS estimation with a large set of covariates (at least 10 or more, as used here), including covariates indirectly related to the outcome, yields better PS balance between treatment and control groups (Stuart & Rubin, 2008). Third, most of the covariates selected here have been used extensively in prior research to understand student academic success and enrollment persistence (Astin, 1993; Pascarella & Terenzini, 2005). More recently, several observational studies that explored causal inference between a select academic experience and a related outcome relied on variables for PS estimation that are largely congruent with those chosen here (Attewell & Domina, 2008; Attewell et al., 2012; Doyle, 2009; Long, Conger, & Iatarola, 2012). For example, Hansen (2004) selected 27 pretreatment variables that capture pretest scores, sociodemographic attributes, academic preparation, and a student's first choice of college to estimate the effect of test preparation courses on math proficiency. Clark and Cundiff (2011) relied on high school GPA, ACT test scores, student ethnicity, motivation indicators, and preference for the institution that were among 19 covariates for PS estimation to gauge the impact of a first-year experience course on GPA and enrollment persistence. Among the variables used here, test date and delayed entry are proxy indicators for student commitment and motivation, following a previous study that used admission date for that purpose (Pike, Hansen, & Lin, 2011).

The covariate-adjusted model that regresses the outcome on the PS and treatment indicator also controls for whether a student took math, English, an online distance education course, visited the on-campus student diversity center, or worked on campus (all coded as dummy variables). However, they cannot be considered pretreatment covariates, as it is possible that the student may have selected into or opted out of these experiences *after* using the services of the math tutoring center. Adding posttreatment variables may mitigate bias in the estimated outcome (Titus, 2007). This method assumes that the covariance between the PS and the outcome is correctly modeled.

PS Methods.   The effect of student use of the math tutoring center on academic momentum and persistence is estimated with several PS-matching algorithms, application of the PS in IPTW, and inclusion of the PS in covariate-adjusted regression. Results of each PS method are estimates of the ATT—that is, the effect on math center users had they not used it—and are compared to standard regression with the same set of covariates. Data were matched using the nearest neighbor, optimal, and full matching functions in the MatchIt R program (Ho, Imai, King, & Stuart, 2011), and genetic matching in R using the Matching program by Sekhon (2011). With IPTW, treated cases receive a weight of 1, while all control cases are weighted on $(P_i(X))/(1-P_i(X))$, where $P_i(X)$ is the PS of the control case, thereby magnifying untreated cases that resemble more closely the treated cases.

With the focus set on the ATT, the common support area is defined by the PS range of treated cases that are matched with untreated (control) cases on the basis of the selected algorithm. The nearest neighbor with replacement (NNR:1) match chooses only the control case with the closest PS to a treated case, and thus the same control case may be matched to multiple treated cases to minimize the average difference (distance) in the PS. This type of matching is suitable for PS distributions with limited overlap between treated and control cases, and where the latter are fewer in number. The second nearest neighbor matching method (NN5:1) uses up to five control cases in random order that fall within 0.2 standard deviations of the PS for each treated case. Austin (2011b) found that the selected caliper width minimizes the mean square error (*MSE*) in the estimated treatment effect if some of the covariates are continuous, as is the case here. The two ways of matching illustrate the potential trade-off between bias and variance, as the replacement method discards control cases that produce poor matches, while the caliper method reduces variance by retaining more control cases that are suitable counterfactuals.

In contrast to nearest neighbor matching, optimal matching minimizes the total within pair or caliper PS difference across all matched pairs. Again, given the bias-variance trade-off, both a one-to-one (Optimal1:1) and a four-to-one (Optimal4:1) control-to-treated ratio were applied. A third variation of optimal matching relied on the Mahalanobis distance measure to determine the selection of control cases in a five-to-one ratio (Mahalanobis5:1). The Mahalanobis is the multidimensional equivalent to the more familiar z-score and works well with a many-to-one ratio and fewer covariates (Rubin, 1980).

An extension of the more commonly used matching by PS stratification is the method of full matching (Full), algorithmically automated to minimize the PS difference by partitioning the data into an optimal number of subclasses that contain the best bidirectional ratio of treated and control cases. The last two matching methods rely on a genetic search algorithm designed to maximize the PS balance across all covariates. Balance is determined with paired t tests for dichotomous variables and the Kolmogorov–Smirnov test for continuous variables at every iteration. The first method (Genetic) lets the evolutionary algorithm automatically adjust the number of cases used in the random trail to meet operator restrictions in order to optimize the solution. The second method (Gen:P1K) sets the number of cases at 1,000 to capitalize on the asymptotic nature of the balancing solution. For further details on these matching algorithms, see Sekhon (2011) and Ho et al. (2011).

Results.   Table 2.1 lists the effect of student use of the math tutoring center estimated with standard parametric regression (first column) versus IPTW and matching on the treated (ATT). Effects on fall and spring momentum are expressed in terms of change on the 100-point scale. The estimated effect on spring and second-year enrollment is expressed as the percentage change associated with the use of the math center vis-à-vis the baseline reference category, students who did not use the math center,

Table 2.1. Estimation of Math Tutoring Effect: Standard Regression Versus Propensity Score Stratification, Matching, and Reweighting

Treated Untreated	OLS/Logit Regression (N = 780) (N = 4,107)*	IPTW (N = 780) (N = 4,107)*	NNR:1 (N = 780) (N = 651)*	NN5:1 (N = 780) (N = 3,528)	Optimal1:1 (N = 780) (N = 780)	Optimal4:1 (N = 780) (N = 3,120)	Mahalanobis5:1 (N = 780) (N = 3,900)	Full:Opt Subcl W (N = 780) (N = 4,107)	Genetic (N = 780) (N = 680)	Gen:P1K (N = 780) (N = 677)	Difference to Standard Regression (A)	Difference to Standard Regression (B)
Fall momentum	**4.1** (0.673)	**4.0** (1.044)	**3.8** (0.636)	**3.8** (0.636)	**8.7** (1.148)	**4.6** (0.913)	**4.4** (0.891)	**7.7** (0.758)	**4.0** (1.103)	**4.5** (1.113)	0.9	−0.2
Spring retention	**6.1%** (1.2)	**3.6%** (1.2)	**3.2%** (1.3)	**3.7%** (0.9)	**6.9%** (1.3)	**4.3%** (1.1)	**3.8%** (1.0)	**6.1%** (0.9)	**3.7%** (1.3)	**4.6%** (1.3)	−1.7%	−2.4%
Spring momentum~	**2.1** (0.468)	**1.9** (0.673)	**2.0** (0.432)	**1.9** (0.442)	**3.3** (0.746)	**1.9** (0.560)	**2.0** (0.545)	**2.8** (0.508)	**1.4** (0.705)	**2.0** (0.707)	0.0	−0.4
Second-year retention	**7.9%** (1.8)	**6.1%** (1.9)	2.3% (1.9)	**6.4%** (1.4)	**11.0%** (2.0)	**7.1%** (1.6)	**6.5%** (1.5)	**10.6%** (1.4)	**5.8%** (2.0)	**5.4%** (1.9)	−1.1%	−1.8%

Bold = significance at 0.05 alpha; *weighted N = 780; ~only retained students. Standard errors in parentheses are bootstrapped (1,000 replications), except for NNR:1 and NN5:1 that use Lechner's formula.

Note: Retention logit coefficients are converted to Delta-*p* percentage points.

applying Cruce's (2009) corrected Delta-p statistic. Standard errors for nearest neighbor matched samples (NNR:1, NN5:1) are based on Lechner's (1999) variance approximation:

$$\frac{1}{N_1} Var(Y(1)|D = 1) + \frac{\sum^i \{D = 0\} (W_i)^2}{N_1} * Var(Y(0)|D = 0),$$

where N_1 is the number of matched treated cases and W_i is the number of repeat uses of a control case when matching with replacement.

All PS methods managed to retain every treated case due to a substantial overlap in the PS distribution between the treated and control group. Figure 2.1 depicts the before- and after-match PS distribution (exemplified with Optimal1:1 matching) and shows improved PS correspondence between treated and control cases at the low and high ends of the PS scale. Visual proof of balance across individual covariates was obtained with quantile plots as exemplified in Figure 2.2. The closer the data points cluster

Figure 2.1. PS Distribution (Optimal1:1)

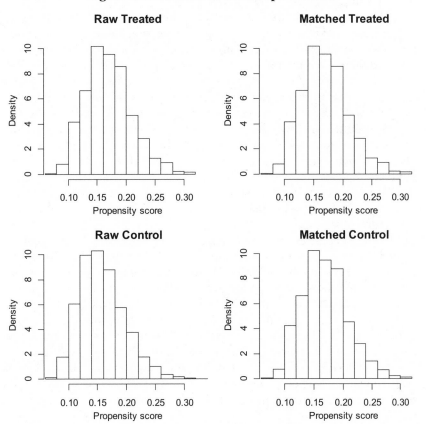

Figure 2.2. Covariate Balance: High School Percentile Rank (QQ Plot for GenP1K Algorithm)

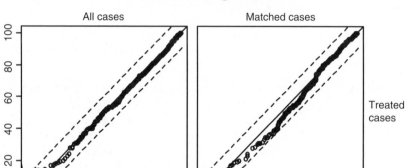

around the 45-degree axis, the greater the balance between the treated and control groups.

The difference in effect size between the average of all nine PS methods and standard regression is listed in column A of Table 2.1. On average, the estimated effect on fall momentum was 20% higher with PS weighted or matched samples compared to standard regression (first column, Table 2.1). The positive effect of student exposure to math tutoring would be underestimated without attempting to reduce selection bias. However, the extent of deviation from the true effect under randomization depends on how well the PS accounts for the probability of treatment selection and the covariate balance achieved in the resampled data. As Table 2.1 shows, the effect size for all outcomes varies across the PS method, with optimal (1:1 ratio) and full matching producing effect sizes that are noticeably higher compared to standard regression. In contrast, the estimated effect obtained with nearest neighbor matching with replacement (NNR:1) is lower compared to standard regression.

Since PS application is predicated on forming a control group of untreated students that is comparable in observed characteristics to the treated students, a comparison of effect size with standard regression must consider the covariate balance between the treated and control groups obtained with each PS estimator. Given the finding by Steiner et al. (2010) that pretest proficiency and student subject preference largely account for bias reduction, Table 2.2 compares the standardized difference in the balance of covariates that are associated with student motivation and education goal (including delayed entry, admission test date, parent education level, plans to go to graduate school, and institution choice) and in the balance of the score on the ACT/SAT math test. These are variables more closely related to those in the Steiner et al. (2010) study. The IPTW, nearest neighbor

Table 2.2. Covariate and Propensity Score Balance

Standardized Difference in Mean for:	IPTW	NNR:1	NN5:1	Optimal1:1	Optimal4:1	Mahalanobis5:1	Full	Genetic	Gen:P1K
All covariates	0.0003	−0.0145	0.0029	−0.1165	−0.0145	0.0009	−0.0986	0.0046	−0.0021
Balance improvement %	91.9	−25.9	77.8	−1183.6	−113.6	16.2	−952.6	9.4	0.2
Motivation, educational goal	−0.0007	−0.0459	0.0014	−0.0463	0.0089	0.0354	−0.0516	−0.0038	−0.0087
Balance improvement %	93.2	−48.2	81.2	−1138.1	−107.1	20.8	−998.8	−13.4	23.7
Math test score	0.0025	−0.0464	0.0068	−0.0265	−0.0075	−0.0890	−0.0351	−0.0223	−0.0131
Balance improvement %	97.8	66.1	95.1	80.7	94.5	35.0	74.4	83.7	90.4
Propensity score	−0.0071	0.0001	0.0107	0.0000	0.0336	−0.1072	−0.0006	0.0488	0.0268
Balance improvement %	96.8	100.0	96.2	100.0	88.1	85.4	99.8	82.7	90.5
Covariates with SD > 0.2	0	0	0	8	0	0	6	0	0
Covariates with SD > 0.1	0	0	0	15	0	0	15	0	0
Covariates with SD > 0.05	0	5	0	20	7	7	18	1	3

(5:1 ratio), and optimal (4:1 ratio) PS estimators yield the best balance for these covariates, while both genetic algorithms produced good balance for covariates related to motivation and education goal. Though all methods improved the balance in the PS by close to 90% or more, four did so by worsening the average covariate balance. Two of those—the Optimal1:1 and the full matching method—failed to achieve the recommended standardized difference of less than 0.10 for most of the included covariates (Austin, 2011b).

In contrast, the IPTW, the nearest neighbor (5:1 ratio), and the genetic algorithm with automatic case selection offer the best balance both among key covariates and overall. Of these three methods, the nearest neighbor matching capitalizes on the large pool of control cases and thus produces the smallest standard errors for all outcomes, including those estimated with regression covariate adjustment (see Table 2.3). The IPTW method is the easiest to execute, requiring merely reweighting of the control cases without applying a matching algorithm. But results from IPTW are more directly affected by the PS weight applied to each case and, by extension, the covariate selection that governs PS estimation. On the other hand, PS matching with multiple control cases smoothes out the PS difference or drops poorly matched cases altogether.

The average estimated effect on fall momentum using the IPTW, the nearest neighbor (5:1 ratio), and the genetic algorithm methods is now lower than the coefficient estimated with standard regression (Table 2.1, column B). Results from the regression covariate adjustment models indicate that the average effect obtained with the three PS methods (Table 2.3, column B) is slightly higher for fall momentum and lower for spring momentum compared to standard regression. Limiting the analysis to only the three PS models with the most balanced covariates produces a lower average effect size compared to the average of all nine PS methods (Table 2.3, column A). Thus, the ATT effect estimated with the PS very much depends on the quality of the covariate balance between the treated and control groups. This finding shows that PS analysis should proceed only after careful covariate balance checks (as recommended in Caliendo & Kopeinig, 2008). While the covariate balance for the optimal (Optimal1:1) and full matching methods may have benefited from inclusion of interaction and higher order terms, this was omitted in order to conduct a comparison of PS methods with identical sets of covariates.

The smaller effect size with the three most balanced PS estimators suggests that standard regression overstates the ATT effect on academic momentum in three of the four measured outcomes (Tables 2.1 and 2.3, column B). The magnitude for standard regression is between 5 and 25% larger. Results for enrollment persistence parallel those for academic momentum. The three PS methods with the best balance across key covariates and overall balance (IPTW, NN5:1, and Genetic) show smaller effects on spring and second-year retention compared to average effects that give equal weight to

Table 2.3. Estimation of Math Tutoring Effect: Regression Covariate Adjustment

Treated Untreated	OLS/Logit Regression (N = 780) (N = 4,107)	IPTW (N = 780) (N = 4,107)*	NNR:1 (N = 780) (N = 651)	NN5:1 (N = 780) (N = 3,528)	Optimal1:1 (N = 780) (N = 780)	Optimal4:1 (N = 780) (N = 3,120)	Mahalanobis5:1 (N = 780) (N = 3,900)	Full (N = 780) (N = 4,107)	Genetic (N = 780) (N = 680)	Gen:P1K (N = 780) (N = 677)	Difference to Standard Regression (A)	Difference to Standard Regression (B)
Fall momentum	**3.4** (0.678)	**3.3** (0.937)	**3.5** (1.102)	**3.5** (0.884)	**8.2** (1.126)	**4.2** (0.920)	**3.6** (1.062)	**7.2** (0.998)	**3.8** (1.094)	**4.1** (1.100)	1.2	0.13
Spring retention	**4.9%** (1.4)	**4.2%** (1.3)	**3.7%** (1.3)	**5.0%** (1.3)	**10.3%** (1.7)	**6.0%** (1.3)	**4.4%** (1.3)	**10.2%** (1.6)	**5.0%** (1.3)	**5.5%** (1.4)	1.1%	−0.2%
Spring momentum~	**1.7** (0.426)	**1.5** (0.551)	**1.6** (0.604)	**1.6** (0.461)	**1.7** (0.647)	**1.4** (0.477)	**1.5** (0.603)	**1.5** (0.488)	1.1 (0.603)	**1.3** (0.616)	−0.2	−0.27
Second-year retention	**5.3%** (1.8)	**4.6%** (2.1)	0.1% (2.0)	**5.6%** (1.8)	**7.3%** (2.3)	**5.8%** (1.9)	**5.2%** (2.1)	**9.1%** (2.0)	3.5% (2.2)	2.7% (2.1)	−0.4%	−0.7%

Bold = significance at 0.05 alpha; *weighted N =780; ~only retained students. Standard errors in parentheses are bootstrapped (1,000 replications), except for NNR:1 and NN5:1 that use Lechner's formula.

First-semester posttreatment covariates: no English, no math, distance education course, worked on campus, used diversity center.

Second-semester posttreatment covariates: as above plus first-semester credits dropped, first-semester I/W/F grades (flag).

Note: Retention logit coefficients are converted to Delta-*p* percentage points.

all nine PS estimators (column A vs. B in Tables 2.1 and 2.3). The average effect size for the three methods with the best covariate balance is consistently lower compared with standard regression (Tables 2.1 and 2.3, column B). Conversely, the largest estimated effects are associated with PS estimators with the poorest covariate balance (Optimal1:1 and Full). These PS estimators may have been more effective with greater covariate imbalance in the raw, unmatched data. Using full matching on a sample of 4,000 students to gauge the impact of coaching on math proficiency, Hansen (2004) was able to remove any significant bias along 27 covariates. The standardized difference in means for the unmatched data ranged from 0.1 to 0.4 for the reported covariates. In contrast, the standard difference in the unmatched data used here is substantially smaller, ranging from 0.01 to 0.09 across covariates.

Whether the difference to standard regression can be attributed to reduced selection bias with the PS weighted and matched data depends on how well the observable characteristics included in the PS estimator capture the process of students choosing to receive math tutoring. As Reynolds and DesJardins (2010) point out in their assessment of the PS approach, calculation of the true treatment effect requires "that the CIA [Conditional Independence Assumption] has been satisfied and that there is no additional selection based on unobservable characteristics" (p. 90). One assumes that selection of the covariates to estimate the PS is sufficient to render the likelihood of math tutoring uncorrelated with academic momentum and enrollment persistence for students who never received math tutoring.

Application of multiple PS methods in a single study helps the institutional research practitioner approximate the true treatment effect, if covariate balance is established on observables that render unconfoundedness plausible. The results here suggest that standard regression overstates the positive impact of the math tutoring center on student academic momentum and enrollment persistence. Unlike standard regression that uses all students in the sampled data for effect estimation, PS matching calculates the effect size with only those students who represent a plausible counterfactual. Thus, the finding of a lower effect size relies only on the three PS methods with a very close balance ($SD \leq 0.05$) on all covariates between the treated and control groups. In particular, covariates associated with student motivation, educational goals, and pretreatment subject proficiency exhibit a nearly identical distribution ($SD \leq 0.01$) across the treated and control groups. These covariates are related to characteristics that explained most of the selection bias in a study on the effect of math training, as demonstrated empirically in Steiner et al. (2010). The smaller effects obtained with PS methods echo findings in comparable studies that found reduced effects with PS-matched data compared to results from unmatched samples (Grunwald & Mayhew, 2008; Long et al., 2012; Reynolds & DesJardins, 2010; Schudde, 2011).

The estimated effect sizes draw on counterfactuals that are matched with the entire sample of treated students. None of the PS matching methods forced deletion of treated cases from the analysis due to lack of common support. Thus, the results are more likely to hold for first-year students in general. The findings suggest that students who used the math tutoring center accrued an academic benefit (in terms of grades, credits earned, and enrollment persistence) that would not have occurred otherwise. Although identification of treated students does not depend on accuracy of self-reports, but instead relies on a verifiable administrative log of student use of the tutoring center, measuring student use as a dichotomous variable does not necessarily capture the nature or intensity of the tutoring service provided. Similarly, a different effect may have emerged with a more direct outcome measure (e.g., math grades instead of GPA) or with covariates in the PS estimation that better control for student subject preference (e.g., indicator of a math-intensive major).

Conclusion

Extensive results from student survey data show a negative relationship between tutoring exposure and grades (Astin, 1993), but this says little about a causal link. The PS method attempts to establish that causal link by reducing the variation in distribution across many pretreatment characteristics to a single metric on which to pair tutored students with the appropriate counterfactual. Since most IR practitioners are not in a position to conduct randomized control studies, the PS method offers an alternative for causal inference estimation between a student-selected campus experience and academic outcomes of interest. The results here show that the PS-based counterfactual framework estimates smaller positive effects on student outcomes than the corresponding standard regression approach. This finding hinges on counterfactuals that closely match "treated" students on observable characteristics that are believed to adequately capture the treatment selection process. To this end, effects from standard regression are compared to PS methods that yield the best covariate balance both overall and on variables that likely account for most of the selection bias. The importance of settling on the PS method that offers the best covariate balance on key variables for bias reduction builds on previous research that benefited from within-study experimental benchmarks.

The finding here draws on sample data that show a large overlap in the PS distribution between the treated and control groups with no reduction in the common support area due to unmatched treated cases, which should render the results more representative of the institutional population. To assist the institutional research practitioner with the application of the PS method, the illustrated example relies on data that are typically available through the student matriculation system, and the discussion focuses on select technical issues on covariate balance and outcome variance estimation that emerged in the PS literature.

References

Abadie, A., & Imbens, G. W. (2008). Notes and comments: On the failure of the bootstrap for matching estimators. *Econometrica, 76,* 1537–1557.

Adelman, C. (2006). *The toolbox revisited: Paths to degree completion from high school through college.* Washington, DC: U.S. Department of Education.

Angrist, J. D. (2003). *Randomized trials and quasi-experiments in education research* (NBER Reporter, No. 4). Cambridge, MA: National Bureau of Economic Research.

Astin, A. W. (1993). *What matters in college? Four critical years revisited.* San Francisco, CA: Jossey-Bass.

Attewell, P., & Domina, T. (2008). Raising the bar: Curricular intensity and academic performance. *Educational Evaluation and Policy Analysis, 30,* 51–71.

Attewell, P., Heil, S., & Reisel, L. (2012). What is academic momentum? And does it matter? *Educational Evaluation and Policy Analysis, 34,* 27–44.

Austin, P. C. (2008). A critical appraisal of propensity-score matching in the medical literature between 1996 and 2003. *Statistics in Medicine, 27,* 2037–2049.

Austin, P. C. (2011a). An introduction to propensity score methods for reducing the effects of confounding in observational studies. *Multivariate Behavioral Research, 46,* 399–424.

Austin, P. C. (2011b). Optimal caliper widths for propensity-score matching when estimating differences in means and differences in proportions in observational studies. *Pharmaceutical Statistics, 10,* 150–161.

Bai, H. (2011). Using propensity score analysis for making causal claims in research articles. *Educational Psychology Review, 23,* 273–278.

Black, D. A., & Smith, J. A. (2004). How robust is the evidence on the effects of college quality? Evidence from matching. *Journal of Econometrics, 121,* 99–124.

Brand, J. E., & Halaby, C. H. (2006). Regression and matching estimates of the effects of elite college attendance on educational and career achievement. *Social Science Research, 35,* 749–770.

Brand, J. E., & Xie, Y. (2010). Who benefits most from college? Evidence for negative selection in heterogeneous economic returns to higher education. *American Sociological Review, 75,* 273–302.

Caliendo, M., & Kopeinig, S. (2008). Some practical guidance for the implementation of propensity score matching. *Journal of Economic Surveys, 22,* 31–72.

Clark, M. H., & Cundiff, N. L. (2011). Assessing the effectiveness of a college freshman seminar using propensity score adjustments. *Research in Higher Education, 52,* 616–639.

Cook, T. D., Steiner, P. M., & Pohl, S. (2009). How bias reduction is affected by covariate choice, unreliability, and mode of data analysis: Results from two types of within-study comparisons. *Multivariate Behavioral Research, 44,* 828–847.

Cruce, T. M. (2009). A note on the calculation and interpretation of the Delta-p statistic for categorical independent variables. *Research in Higher Education, 50,* 608–622.

Doyle, W. R. (2009). The effects of community college enrollment on bachelor's degree completion. *Economics of Education Review, 28,* 199–206.

Gangl, M. (2010). Causal inference in sociological research. *Annual Review of Sociology, 36,* 21–47.

Grunwald, H. E., & Mayhew, M. J. (2008). Using propensity scores for estimating causal effects: A study in the development of moral reasoning. *Research in Higher Education, 49,* 758–775.

Hansen, B. B. (2004). Full matching in an observational study of coaching for the SAT. *Journal of the American Statistical Association, 99*, 609–618.

Harder, V. S., Stuart, E. A., & Anthony, J. C. (2010). Propensity score techniques and the assessment of measured covariate balance to test causal associations in psychological research. *Psychological Methods, 15*, 234–249.

Heckman, J. J. (2000). Causal parameters and policy analysis in economics: A twentieth century retrospective. *The Quarterly Journal of Economics, 115*, 45–97.

Herzog, S. (2008, January). *Estimating the influence of financial aid on student retention* (Education Working Paper Archive). Fayetteville, AR: University of Arkansas, Department of Education Reform.

Ho, D. E., Imai, K., King, G., & Stuart, E. (2011). MatchIt: Nonparametric preprocessing for parametric causal inference. *Journal of Statistical Software, 42*(8), 1–28.

Holland, P. W. (1986). Statistics and causal inference. *Journal of the American Statistical Association, 81*, 945–960.

Lechner, M. (1999, December). *Identification and estimation of causal effects of multiple treatments under the conditional independence assumption* (Discussion Paper No. 91). Bonn, Germany: Institute for the Study of Labor (IZA).

Long, M. C., Conger, D., & Iatarola, P. (2012). Effects of high school course-taking on secondary and postsecondary success. *American Educational Research Journal, 49*, 285–322.

Luellen, J. K., Shadish, W. R., & Clark, M. H. (2005). Propensity scores: An introduction and experimental test. *Evaluation Review, 29*, 530–558.

Melguizo, T., Kienzl, G. S., & Alfonso, M. (2011). Comparing the educational attainment of community college transfer students and four-year college rising juniors using propensity score matching methods. *The Journal of Higher Education, 82*, 265–291.

Morgan, S. L., & Harding, D. J. (2006). Matching estimators of causal effects: Prospects and pitfalls in theory and practice. *Sociological Methods & Research, 35*, 3–60.

Morgan, S. L., & Winship, C. (2007). *Counterfactuals and causal inference: Methods and principles for social research.* New York, NY: Cambridge University Press.

Murnane, R. J., & Willett, J. B. (2010). *Methods matter: Improving causal inference in educational and social science research.* New York, NY: Oxford University Press.

Olitsky, N. H. (2014). How do academic achievement and gender affect the earnings of STEM majors? A propensity score matching approach. *Research in Higher Education, 55*(3), 245–271.

Pascarella, E. T., & Terenzini, P. T. (2005). *How college affects students: A third decade of research.* San Francisco, CA: Jossey-Bass.

Pearl, J. (2000). Causal inference without counterfactuals: Comment. *Journal of the American Statistical Association, 95*, 428–431.

Pike, G. R., Hansen, M. J., & Lin, C. (2011). Using instrument variables to account for selection effects in research on first-year programs. *Research in Higher Education, 52*, 194–214.

Reynolds, C. L., & DesJardins, S. L. (2010). The use of matching methods in higher education research. In J. C. Smart (Ed.), *Higher education: Handbook of theory and research* (Vol. 24; pp. 47–104). New York, NY: Springer.

Rosenbaum, P. R. (2002). *Observational studies.* New York, NY: Springer.

Rosenbaum, P. R., & Rubin, D. B. (1983). The central role of the propensity score in observational studies for causal effects. *Biometrika, 70*, 41–55.

Rosenbaum, P. R., & Rubin, D. B. (1984). Reducing bias in observational studies using subclassification on the propensity score. *Journal of the American Statistical Association, 79*, 516–524.

Rubin, D. B. (1980). Bias reduction using Mahalanobis metric matching. *Biometrics, 36*, 293–298.

Rubin, D. B. (2006). *Matched sampling for causal inference.* New York, NY: Cambridge University Press.

Rubin, D. B., & Thomas, N. (1996). Matching using estimated propensity scores, relating theory to practice. *Biometrics, 52,* 249–264.

Rubin, D. B., & Thomas, N. (2000). Combining propensity score matching with additional adjustments for prognostic covariates. *Journal of the American Statistical Association, 95,* 573–585.

Schudde, L. T. (2011). The causal effect of campus residency on college student retention. *The Review of Higher Education, 34,* 581–610.

Sekhon, J. S. (2011). Multivariate and propensity score matching software with automated balance optimization: The Matching package for R. *Journal of Statistical Software, 42*(7), 1–22.

Shadish, W. R. (2013). Propensity score analysis: Promise, reality and irrational exuberance. *Journal of Experimental Criminology, 9,* 129–144.

Steiner, P. M., Cook, T. D., Shadish, W. R., & Clark, M. H. (2010). The importance of covariate selection in controlling for selection bias in observational studies. *Psychological Methods, 15,* 250–267.

Stuart, E. A. (2008). Commentary: Developing practical recommendations for the use of propensity scores. *Statistics in Medicine, 27,* 2062–2065.

Stuart, E. A. (2010). Matching methods for causal inference: A review and look forward. *Statistical Science, 25,* 1–21.

Stuart, E. A., & Rubin, D. B. (2008). Best practices in quasi-experimental designs. In J. W. Osborne (Ed.), *Best practices in quantitative methods* (pp. 155–176). Thousand Oaks, CA: Sage.

Thoemmes, F. J., & Kim, E. S. (2011). A systematic review of propensity score methods in the social sciences. *Multivariate Behavioral Research, 46,* 90–118.

Titus, M. A. (2007). Detecting selection bias, using propensity score matching, and estimating treatment effects. *Research in Higher Education, 48,* 487–521.

U.S. Department of Education. (2003). *Identifying and implementing educational practices supported by rigorous evidence: A user friendly guide.* Washington, DC: Institute of Education Sciences.

SERGE HERZOG *is director of institutional analysis at the University of Nevada, Reno.*

3

Item Response Theory (IRT) is a measurement theory that is ideal for scale and test development in institutional research, but it is not without its drawbacks. This chapter provides an overview of IRT, describes an example of its use, and highlights the pros and cons of using IRT in applied settings.

Item Response Theory: Overview, Applications, and Promise for Institutional Research

Jessica Sharkness

Introduction

One of the more difficult tasks facing researchers in higher education is the measurement of difficult-to-observe, multifaceted student experiences and outcomes. Many of the phenomena of interest to higher education researchers, such as student involvement, critical thinking, and civic engagement, cannot be measured directly because they are theoretical in nature and therefore unobservable. Such phenomena, also called *latent traits* or *latent constructs* (Embretson & Reise, 2000), must be measured indirectly using indicators that *are* observable, and that are thought to be influenced by the latent constructs. In higher education, the indicators that are typically used to measure latent constructs are test and survey questions. For example, one might design a measure of student engagement by developing a bank of survey items asking about a variety of activities that represent manifestations of engagement. By observing students' responses to these items, one can infer the "level" of engagement exhibited by these students. Or one might design a test of critical thinking that consists of a series of questions that are thought to elicit responses demonstrating students' ability to think critically. On the basis of answers to the questions, one can make an estimate of students' "levels" of critical thinking.

In order to determine "levels" of a latent trait on the basis of responses to a set of items, what is called a *measurement theory* must be used. As Allen and Yen (1979/2000) write, *measurement* is "the assigning of numbers to individuals in a systematic way as a means of representing properties of the individuals" (p. 2). *Measurement theory* is a type of applied statistics that

NEW DIRECTIONS FOR INSTITUTIONAL RESEARCH, no. 161 © 2014 Wiley Periodicals, Inc.
Published online in Wiley Online Library (wileyonlinelibrary.com) • DOI: 10.1002/ir.20066

41

aims to "describe, categorize, and evaluate the quality of measurements, improve the usefulness, accuracy, and meaningfulness of measurements, and propose methods for developing new and better measurements" (p. 2). In the social sciences, two primary measurement theories are used to develop, score, and evaluate scales and tests: Classical Test Theory (CTT) and Item Response Theory (IRT). Although not usually explicitly stated, most extant measurement in higher education has relied almost exclusively on CTT (Sharkness & DeAngelo, 2011). However, since CTT was developed, the much more sophisticated IRT has been quietly and rapidly gaining ground (Embretson & Reise, 2000).

Institutional researchers may frequently face situations in which it is necessary to produce measurements of complex constructs. Student surveys, for instance, are often designed to access complex student experiences and outcomes, such as student involvement, self-confidence, satisfaction, and attitudes toward campus climate. On the academic side, outcomes assessments often involve the development of test or rubric items that, as a group, are intended to measure a specific skill or set of skills. While it can be useful to examine items on such surveys and tests on an individual basis, it can be even more instructive to employ a measurement theory to assess how the items interrelate with one another, how well the items measure the intended construct, and how students compare to one another in terms of their "levels" of the underlying construct. In addition, measurement theories can be quite profitably used to assess the reliability and validity of existing survey and test instruments, as well as to provide suggestions for improvement of the instruments.

IRT is ideal for measuring the latent constructs of interest in institutional research. Not only does it produce estimates of abilities or traits that do not depend on one specific set of items, but it also provides rich information about measurement precision that can be used to make data-driven, theoretically defensible improvements to surveys and tests. However, IRT is also more complicated than CTT and can therefore be harder to employ, interpret, and explain. This chapter begins with a basic overview of IRT, including a brief comparison of IRT and CTT. The chapter then provides an example of how IRT has been used by higher education researchers to develop and assess a scale measuring student–faculty interaction. The chapter concludes with a brief discussion of some challenges of using IRT in applied settings like institutional research.

Introduction to Classical Test Theory and Item Response Theory

Because latent traits are unobservable, researchers must measure them indirectly through instruments such as tests, tasks, or surveys.[1] Typically, an instrument designed to measure a particular latent construct will contain a series of items that content experts believe tap into various aspects of the construct. CTT and IRT are both tools that can be used to assess the appropriateness of such item sets and to evaluate instruments as a whole. However, the two theories make very different assumptions about the nature of the construct being measured and about how individuals respond to tests and surveys. In this section, some basic tenets of CTT and IRT are described. Note that this summary is not intended to cover every nuance of IRT or CTT; for more detailed discussions see Allen and Yen (1979/2000) on CTT and Embretson and Reise (2000) on IRT. Embretson and Reise also provide a thorough theoretical comparison of CTT and IRT, while Sharkness and DeAngelo (2011) provide an empirical comparison of the two theories in the context of higher education.

In CTT, a person's observed score on a test or instrument is assumed to be equal to some "true" score plus random error. The true score is a theoretical concept defined as the expected mean of a hypothetical distribution of scores that would be obtained if the same person were given the same test over a series of repeated and independent observations (Allen & Yen, 1979/2000). Error is defined as the random, unsystematic deviations from the true score that occur in each of the (theoretical) observations. For any given person and test, it is assumed that true score will not vary over repeated observations, but observed score and error will. It is important to note that these definitions imply that a person's "true" score is "true" only for one specific test or scale—if a different set of items were developed to measure the same construct, each individual would have a different "true" score for the new item set, and his or her observed scores and errors would consequently differ as well.

Individuals cannot in reality be administered the same instrument repeatedly and independently, so CTT can never disentangle true score and error at the person level. The only way to estimate the psychometric properties of a test in CTT—including the standard error of measurement (SEM)—is by using observations from a group of people. Clearly, for any given test, the composition of the group of people used to calibrate it and the specific items it contains will have a large bearing on the CTT statistics that are observed. As a result, CTT statistics and their interpretation are always dependent on a particular set of items and a particular population.[2] In addition, to be able to estimate the SEM for a test, CTT assumes that error is random across people and constant across all true scores (Allen & Yen, 1979/2000). Therefore, tests are assumed to be equally accurate for all individuals, even those with very different levels of the latent construct being measured.

Because the fundamental assumptions and equations of CTT focus on the level of the test—true scores and errors relate to a test as a whole, and do not concern the parts that make up the test—the theory makes no provision for the actual calculation of test scores on the basis of item responses (Allen & Yen, 1979/2000; Embretson & Reise, 2000). Test or scale scores in CTT are usually obtained by summing together responses for the items on the test or scale (Embretson & Reise, 2000). This method is simple, but it ensures that properties of items, such as their difficulty, cannot be directly related to the score obtained by an individual (Hambleton & Jones, 1993). That is, if person A correctly answered five questions on a test, and person B correctly answered five different questions, CTT would say that they have the same score (and that their scores are measured with the same degree of precision) regardless of how difficult the items were or how likely it would be for a person with a given ability level to answer those particular questions correctly. Or as Thorpe and Favia (2012) describe, a depression inventory may have 21 questions, each with a four-point response scale (coded 0, 1, 2, or 3), and a score of 14 or above (calculated by summing the responses to each of the 21 questions) may be indicative of at least mild depression. It is easy to see that a patient may score 14 by responding in a wide variety of ways to the 21 questions, so individuals classified as having mild depression may therefore have very different patterns of specific problems or symptoms. Under a CTT framework, there is no way to distinguish among these individuals.

CTT scores are not only difficult to relate back to items, but they are also difficult to compare to one another. Raw scores obtained by summing responses to a set of items have no inherent meaning, so it is difficult to say if a given score is "good" or "bad." To give meaning to raw scores in CTT, some kind of transformation must be applied. Many of the most common transformations are defined with respect to a norm or reference group, such as percentiles and standardized scores (Allen & Yen, 1979/2000). Although norm-referenced transformations make scores much more interpretable, the results of the transformations depend a great deal on the reference group. In addition, norm-referenced calculations like percentiles involve nonlinear calculations, which means that while the order of examinee scores remains the same after the transformation, the distance between the scores does not. Therefore, norm-referenced scores often do not achieve measurement levels greater than ordinal, making common statistics like means and standard deviations—not to mention inferential techniques like ordinary least-squares regression—inappropriate. Although standardized score transformations *are* linear in nature, they too do not necessarily produce the interval-level, normally distributed scores that are assumed by most parametric statistical techniques because the shape of the raw score distribution (which may be quite irregular) is maintained with any linear transformation.

IRT takes a fundamentally different approach to measurement. In contrast to CTT, IRT assumes that the desired construct of measurement exists independently of any particular test or instrument. More formally, IRT assumes that every person has some "true" location on a continuous latent dimension called *theta*, which is assumed to probabilistically influence responses to any item related to the trait (Embretson & Reise, 2000). IRT models theta with mathematical functions that examine responses to a set of items and, controlling for the characteristics of the items, estimate the level of theta that is most likely to yield the observed responses. Embretson and Reise (2000) liken IRT to the process of clinical inference because item responses can be seen as "symptoms of a latent variable that must be inferred" (p. 54), much like a cough, sore throat, and fever are symptoms that can help a doctor infer the presence of influenza. Ostini and Nering (2006) note that IRT models are functions that describe "in probabilistic terms, how a person with a higher standing on a trait (i.e., more of the trait) is likely to provide a response in a different response category to a person with a low standing on the trait" (p. 2). In IRT, there are a variety of mathematical functions that can relate response patterns to theta; the choice of these depends on the nature of the data to be analyzed (Embretson & Reise, 2000; Hambleton & Jones, 1993).

Importantly, item properties in IRT are explicitly incorporated into the modeling procedure, and they exist independently of trait estimates, test instruments, and particular populations of test takers. As a consequence, latent trait scores are not dependent on a specific set of items, as they are in CTT, and properties of items can be modeled separately from properties of tests and people. In IRT, individuals no longer need to be administered the same set of items in order to get comparable scores on a latent trait; once item properties are known, items can be recombined in multiple ways to develop different but comparable measures. In addition, standard errors can vary both for different response patterns and for different levels of the underlying latent trait. Items can therefore be combined strategically to reduce SEM in areas of the latent trait continuum that are of critical interest. Further, assessments of scales and items in IRT are not as easily influenced by the composition of the calibration sample as are CTT assessments. To achieve a good item calibration (and therefore a good assessment of the instrument as a whole), it is only necessary to have a sample that is heterogeneous on the latent trait (Embretson & Reise, 2000).

In contrast to CTT, IRT estimates of latent trait scores are easily interpretable and are also easy to compare across different people and different (calibrated) instruments. The distribution of a latent trait is usually specified before modeling, and in most applications is assumed to have a standard normal distribution, with a mean of 0 and standard deviation of 1 (Embretson & Reise, 2000). Given such an assumption, trait estimates immediately have inherent meaning—positive estimates are above average, for instance, and negative estimates are below average. In addition, the scores have properties that are closer to interval than any raw CTT score could be (Reise, Ainsworth, & Haviland, 2005). IRT also calibrates items and persons on the same scale, so scores can be directly related back to the probability of responding in a particular way to a particular item. To return to the depression example from earlier, under an IRT framework, mild depression could be defined not by an overall score of 14, but rather by actual responses to specific items on the inventory. That is, low scores on the depression scale could be related directly to the symptoms that subjects indicate experiencing, so someone with mild depression could be defined as exhibiting sadness and pessimism, but not self-accusation or suicidal ideation.[3] Individuals with the same raw CTT score no longer need to have the same trait estimate, which likely more accurately reflects reality (Castro, Trentini, & Riboldi, 2010).

IRT Basics

The following few sections provide a basic introduction to IRT, describing some fundamental concepts, including item response functions, item parameters, and psychometric information.

Item Response Functions: The Dichotomous Case.   IRT models item properties using what are called *item response functions* (IRFs), or mathematical functions that describe the relationship between a person's level of a latent trait (theta; again, usually assumed to have a standard normal distribution) and the probability that he or she will respond in a particular way to an item measuring that trait (Reise et al., 2005). Figure 3.1 shows the IRFs of three hypothetical dichotomous items (true/false, yes/no, correct/incorrect). The figure displays on the vertical axis the probability of responding in the positive or *keyed* category (true, yes, correct) as a function

Figure 3.1. Examples of Item Response Functions (IRFs) for Three Dichotomous Items

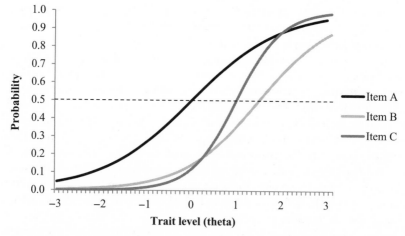

Note: Item A has a difficulty/location (*b*) of 0 and a discrimination (*a*) of 1, Item B has a difficulty/location of 1.5 and a discrimination of 1.2, and Item C has a difficulty/location of 1 and a discrimination of 2.

of theta, which is displayed on the horizontal axis. In IRT terminology, the point on the latent trait continuum where the curve changes direction (the inflection point) is called an item's *difficulty* or its *location*, and is usually represented by a *b*. Individuals with theta levels below an item's *b* are predicted to respond in the *unkeyed* category (false, no, incorrect), whereas individuals with theta levels above *b* are predicted to respond in the keyed direction (true, yes, correct). At theta levels of *b* exactly, individuals have a 50–50 chance of responding in either category. In Figure 3.1, Item A has a difficulty/location of 0, Item B has a difficulty/location of 1.5, and Item C has a difficulty/location of 1. An individual with a latent trait level of 1.2 would be expected to answer in the keyed category (true, yes, correct) for Items A and C (both have locations lower than the person's theta), and in the unkeyed category (false, no, incorrect) for Item B (which has a location greater than the person's theta).

Another characteristic of IRFs that is often modeled in IRT is steepness or slope.[4] The slope parameter, usually represented by an *a* and called an item's *discrimination*, is estimated at the inflection point of each function, where steepness is at its maximum. Item slope parameters give an indication of how well an item discriminates among individuals, particularly individuals with trait levels close to the item's difficulty/location. Items with larger *a* parameters are more discriminating because the probability of responding in the keyed category changes more rapidly as a function of trait level. In Figure 3.1, Item A has a slope of 1, Item B has a slope of 1.2, and Item C has a slope of 2. Item C is therefore the most discriminating item, and it is easy to see why if one looks at the probability of responding in the keyed category to Item C versus Item A at various points on the theta continuum. At the difficulty/location for each item (*b*), individuals are predicted to be equally likely to respond in the keyed category to both Items A and C. At a theta level of $b+0.5$ (half a standard deviation above *b*), individuals have an approximately 62% chance of responding in the keyed category to Item A, but a 73% chance of responding in the keyed category to Item C. Similarly, at a theta level of $b-0.5$ (half a standard deviation below *b*), individuals have a 38% probability of responding in the keyed category to Item A, while for Item C this figure is 27%. Therefore, given a response of "true," "yes," or "correct" to Item C, one can say with greater certainty that this individual likely has a trait level above its *b*.

Operating Characteristic Curves and Category Response Curves: The Polytomous Case. The preceding description concerns the IRFs for dichotomous items, which can be scored true/false, yes/no, or correct/incorrect. IRT is also able to model polytomous items, or items in which a respondent can answer in more than two categories, none of which can be called "correct." In order to be able to model such items, however, IRT must treat the multiple answer categories as a set of concatenated dichotomies (Ostini & Nering, 2006). In higher education settings, the most commonly encountered polytomous items are survey items that have Likert response options, and the IRT model that is typically used with Likert data is Samejima's (1969) graded response model (GRM; Embretson & Reise, 2000; Ostini & Nering, 2006).[5] Under the GRM, the dichotomization of ordered categorical responses occurs at the boundary between each category, so a Likert item with five response categories will have four boundaries to separate them. The dichotomies separating the categories are thought of as representing the probability of a particular individual responding above a particular boundary ("positively") versus in any category below the boundary ("negatively"). When modeled, these dichotomies can be described by what are called *Operating Characteristic Curves* (OCCs; Embretson & Reise, 2000) or *Category Boundary Response Functions* (Ostini & Nering, 2006). Figure 3.2 displays an example of OCCs for a five-category Likert-type item with response options of Strongly Disagree, Disagree, Neutral, Agree, and Strongly Agree. Notably, each of the OCCs can be described in the same way as the curves shown in Figure 3.1, with a slope/discrimination (*a*) and a location (*b*). For the GRM, the slopes of all of the OCCs are fixed to be equivalent, but each OCC has a different "location." In the GRM, the "location" parameters (*b*s) are usually called *threshold* parameters because they represent the threshold between two response categories.

Because the goal of the GRM is to estimate parameters that can describe the probability of an individual responding *in* a particular category, given his or her level of underlying trait, OCCs are usually used simply as stepping stones to get to the final functions of interest, *Category Response Curves*

Figure 3.2. Operating Characteristic Curves or Category Boundary Response Functions for a Five-Category Polytomous Item

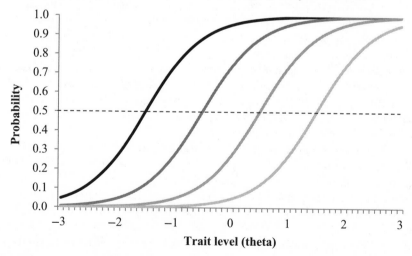

Note: For example, response categories for a five-category polytomous item are strongly disagree, disagree, neutral, agree, and strongly agree.

Figure 3.3. Category Response Curves for a Five-Category Example Item Under the Graded Responses Model

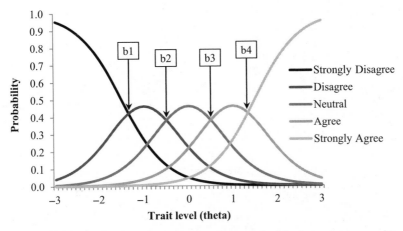

Notes: These curves show the probability of responding in each of the five categories, conditional on theta. The *b*1 through *b*4 threshold parameters represent the point on the latent trait continuum where there is an equal likelihood of responding in a particular response category or above as there is of responding in any other lower category.

(CRCs). CRCs are calculated by "subtracting" the OCCs from one another (Embretson & Reise, 2000), and they show the probability of an individual with a given level of theta responding in each possible category.

Figure 3.3 shows the CRCs associated with the item whose OCCs were modeled in Figure 3.2. Note that for any fixed theta level, there is some probability that an individual will respond in any of the available categories, but there is also usually a single category in which response is most likely. At the lower end of the theta continuum, for example around theta $= -3$, it is quite unlikely that an individual will respond "Strongly Agree" ($p < .01$) and it is overwhelmingly likely that an individual will respond "Strongly Disagree" ($p \approx .95$). In the middle of the theta continuum (around theta $= 0$), an individual is most likely to respond "Neutral" ($p \approx .46$), but he or she also has some likelihood of responding "Agree" ($p \approx .22$) or "Disagree" ($p \approx .22$). At this same point, however, it is relatively unlikely that an individual will respond "Strongly Agree" or "Strongly Disagree" ($p \approx .05$ for both).

Information.   One of the great advantages of IRT over CTT is the intelligence that it provides about measurement precision over the entire latent trait continuum. The way in which this is modeled in IRT is with an *Item Information Function* (IIF), which shows the amount of psychometric information an item contains as a function of theta (Embretson & Reise, 2000). Figure 3.4 shows the IIFs for the three dichotomous items introduced in Figure 3.1. Note that each of the information curves is

Figure 3.4. Item Information Functions (IIFs) for the Three Dichotomous Items Whose IRCs Are Graphed in Figure 3.1

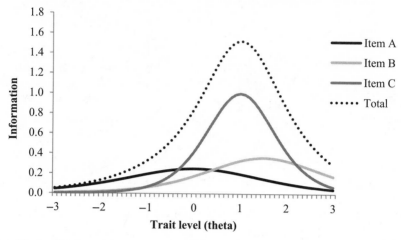

Note: The "total" information represents the sum of the information of Items A through C.

peaked, reflecting the fact that dichotomous items provide the most information immediately around their difficulty/location parameters (bs). In addition, each of the curves has a different height, reflecting the fact that the items' discrimination parameters (their as) are different. Recall that Item A had the smallest discrimination parameter, and Item C the largest. As a consequence, Item A has the flattest information curve, and Item C the most peaked. The curves shown in Figure 3.4 visually demonstrate that Item A provides only a small amount of information spread out along the latent trait continuum. Item C, by contrast, provides much more information, but it is concentrated in a particular area of the continuum.

IIFs are useful for two primary reasons. First, they are additive across items that are calibrated to the same latent trait continuum. Therefore, IIFs for a test or scale can be summed to get a measure of how well the entire scale functions as a measurement of the latent trait—a test-level information curve. The dotted curve in Figure 3.4, for example, shows the total information provided by Items A, B, and C; this curve represents the sum of the three curves underneath it. Second, test-level information can, in turn, be converted into the SEM for the test using a simple formula (one over the square root of total information). Figure 3.5 shows the total information from Figure 3.4, along with the associated SEM across the theta continuum. Note that as information peaks, standard error has its nadir. In addition, SEM is lowest for theta levels close to the items' location parameters. Such a view of SEM contrasts sharply with CTT, in which SEM is assumed constant across all test takers.

Figure 3.5. Information Curve for the Test/Scale Composed of Items A, B, and C Along With the Standard Error of Measurement for This Test/Scale

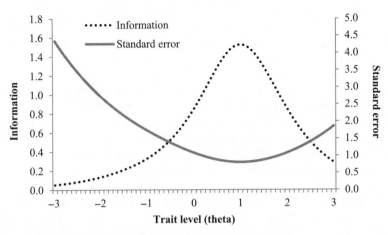

Notes: See Figures 3.1 and 3.4 for more information on Items A, B, and C.
Standard error of measurement is calculated as 1 over the square root of information at each theta.

Information and standard error work in analogous ways for polytomous items as they do for dichotomous items, though IIFs for polytomous items tend to have multiple "peaks," reflecting the multiple dichotomies represented within the item. Because the interpretation of IIFs and test-level information functions is the same for polytomous items as for dichotomous, further discussion of these curves is reserved for the following example.

Item Response Theory in Action: Measuring Student Engagement

IRT can be used by institutional researchers and higher education scholars for a variety of purposes. One of the most fruitful areas in which IRT may be applied is in the development or assessment of survey scales measuring intangible aspects of the college experience, such as sense of belonging, campus climate, and student engagement. Student engagement is of particular interest to many higher education stakeholders, and the number of local and national surveys designed to measure engagement has risen dramatically over the past few decades. While a plethora of survey scales have already been developed to measure engagement of various kinds (see, for example, Astin, 1993; Kuh, 2001), virtually all were developed under the rubric of CTT, and the measures therefore did not benefit from the useful analytics provided by IRT (Sharkness & DeAngelo, 2011).

Around 2007, the Cooperative Institutional Research Program (CIRP) at the Higher Education Research Institute (HERI) launched an initiative to develop scales (or *CIRP Constructs*; CIRP, n.d.) that measure various aspects of the student experience, including interaction with diverse peers, sense of belonging, and academic engagement (CIRP, 2009). Although researchers had already developed a number of multi-item scales using the CIRP surveys, all of these had been created using CTT methods (see, for example, Astin, 1993; Chang, Han, Sàenz, & Cerna, 2008; Hurtado et al., 2007). Therefore, all existing scales suffered from the same drawbacks—the results were inherently sample-dependent, SEM was assumed to be constant across the continuum of the trait being measured, the meaning and scoring of the scales changed when different numbers of items were included, and the scale scores were difficult to meaningfully compare across populations and/or points in time. CIRP decided to use IRT for its construct project to avoid many of these pitfalls, but also because IRT gave CIRP the flexibility to add and remove items from its surveys without altering the meaning or scale of the constructs that had been developed.

In the *CIRP Construct Technical Report*, Sharkness, DeAngelo, and Pryor (2010) describe the process of creating the CIRP Constructs. In the report, the authors provide an example of a faculty–student interaction construct, developed from items on the Your First College Year (YFCY) survey. The report describes the selection of items, the evaluation of the item set, and the estimation of IRT parameters using Samejima's (1969) GRM. In addition, the report covers the assessment of one of the key assumptions of the IRT models discussed in this chapter—the *unidimensionality* of the item set. In brief, the assumption of unidimensionality demands that the items evaluated using IRT all measure the same construct and that construct alone. A thorough exposition of unidimensionality is beyond the scope of this chapter, but see Embretson and Reise (2000) for a discussion of its meaning and importance and Sharkness and DeAngelo (2011) for an example of how it has been assessed for a student engagement scale on the basis of survey data. Here, the final items chosen for the faculty–student interaction construct are borrowed to illustrate the way in which IRT can not only assess scales and items, but also help theory building as a part of scale improvement.

Table 3.1 shows the six items that were chosen for the CIRP YFCY faculty–student interaction construct. The table also shows the discrimination and threshold parameters that were estimated for these items. Item discriminations range from 1.18 (relatively moderate) to 2.71 (very high; Baker, 2001), and threshold parameters fall between −4.34 and 3.60—a good range that spans the trait levels most likely to be observed. The threshold parameters are not evenly spread across the continuum, however, but are rather clustered in particular areas. Specifically, about a third of the threshold parameters (5 of 16) cluster between −1.21 and

Table 3.1. Item Discrimination and Threshold Parameters for the Six Faculty Interaction Items

Item		a	$b1$	$b2$	$b3$	$b4$	$b5$
1	Freq: Interact with faculty outside class/office hours[a]	1.18	−1.17	0.16	1.19	2.21	3.60
2	Freq: Ask a professor for advice after class[b]	1.74	−1.21	1.36			
3	Freq: Communicate regularly with your professors[b]	2.71	−0.90	1.10			
4	Satisfaction: Amount of contact with faculty[c]	1.20	−4.34	−2.76	−0.76	1.59	
5	Freq: Professors provide advice about educational program[b]	1.69	−0.87	1.48			
6	Yes/No: Ever go to office hours[d]	1.29	−2.24				

[a]Six response categories: 6 = Daily, 5 = Two or three times per week, 4 = Once a week, 3 = One or two times per month, 2 = One or two times per term, 1 = Never.
[b]Three response categories: 3 = Frequently, 2 = Occasionally, 1 = Not at all.
[c]Five response categories: 5 = Very satisfied, 4 = Satisfied, 3 = Neutral, 2 = Dissatisfied, 1 = Very dissatisfied.
[d]Two response categories: 1 = Yes, 0 = No.
Source: Reprinted from *CIRP Construct Technical Report* (p. 18) by J. Sharkness, L. DeAngelo, and J. H. Pryor, 2010, Higher Education Research Institute, University of California, Los Angeles.

−0.76, and another quarter (4 of 16) cluster between 1.10 and 1.48. Only one of the threshold values falls between −0.76 and 1.10, but this was in the least discriminating item (Item 1). Clustered item thresholds like these are not ideal for applications in which a broad spectrum of students is to be measured. With only one threshold around zero, the set of items cannot provide much information about students with average—the most likely—faculty interaction levels. However, the items *are* able to make relatively precise estimates of faculty interaction levels for students who are approximately one standard deviation below the mean (theta ≈ −1) as well as for students approximately one standard deviation above the mean (theta ≈ 1).

A look at the item information curves for the faculty interaction scale (Figure 3.6) confirms the conclusions reached by examining the threshold parameters. The psychometric information provided by many of the items, particularly the most discriminating ones, dips noticeably around theta ≈ 0. Not surprisingly, the total scale information dips at the same point, and standard error correspondingly rises (Figure 3.7).

The observed picture of measurement precision for the faculty–student interaction construct presents an interesting challenge to survey developers and researchers at CIRP. The lack of threshold parameters around

Figure 3.6. Item Information Functions for the Six Items in the Faculty–Student Interaction Construct

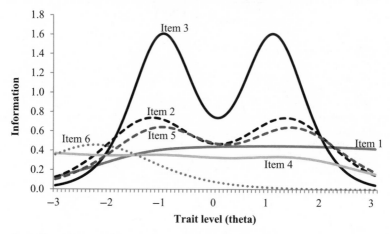

Note: See Table 3.1 for item discrimination and threshold parameters.

zero indicates that the current set of items (and/or response options) does not fully capture how the average first-year student interacts with faculty. The natural question that arises, then, is: why not? Excitingly, this is a question that is best answered by a look at the literature and theory surrounding faculty–student interaction. In order to draft an item that

Figure 3.7. Total Information and SEM

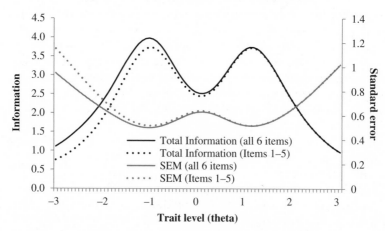

Note: Total information and SEM are provided for all six faculty–student interaction items introduced in Table 3.1 and Figure 3.6, as well as for the set of items without Item 6.

better covers the middle portion of the continuum, fundamental questions must be answered, such as: What are the types of faculty–student interaction that first-year college students typically engage in? What manifestations of the typical student's interaction with faculty are missing from the construct? Might it be problematic that many of the currently included items focus on the amount of contact with faculty (and/or the mode of contact), rather than the "content" of the contact? If so, what kind of "content" might be relevant?

Space can be limited on CIRP surveys, which makes it difficult to add a large number of new items simply to test in the faculty–student interaction construct. Fortunately, IRT provides analytics that can help survey developers like those at CIRP select specific items to remove and replace. IIFs are key tools for this purpose because they can be added and subtracted to show what the scale-level information function would look like if only a subset of items were included. As an example, Figure 3.7 shows the scale-level information function for the faculty–student interaction construct in two scenarios: first, for the full set of items (solid lines), and second, for the set consisting of Items 1 through 5 only (dotted lines). Because Item 6, a dichotomous item, had a location parameter of -2.24, it provides the most psychometric information about students who have faculty interaction levels a little more than two standard deviations below the mean and relatively little information elsewhere (see Figure 3.6). If this item were removed from the YFCY, the total information for the faculty interaction construct would decrease—but only for individuals with faculty interaction levels lower than two standard deviations below the mean. The information provided about students who are average or above average on this construct would remain largely unchanged, since the item provided virtually no information about students in these areas. The scale-level information curve that results with the removal of Item 6 may be acceptable to CIRP's survey developers if the item were replaced with one that better measures the middle portion of the faculty interaction continuum. However, it may equally be unacceptable because the removal of Item 6 increases standard error too much in the lower portion of the continuum, which may be an area of critical interest. If unacceptable, similar graphs may be created that examine the impact of removing each of the other items. On the basis of these graphs, an educated decision can be made about which item is best to remove and replace.

Conclusion

IRT offers a great deal of promise for institutional researchers and others in higher education. It is a powerful and flexible measurement theory that represents a clear improvement over CTT. IRT produces item parameters that are population-independent, latent construct scores that are item-independent, clear ways to relate items to latent traits, an informative view of measurement precision, and scores with desirable measurement properties. However, IRT is not without its drawbacks. IRT models require that many assumptions be met; if these assumptions are violated, difficulties in interpretation will arise (Harvey & Hammer, 1999). Specialized software is also needed; standard statistical packages like SPSS do not have IRT capabilities. But perhaps the biggest drawback of IRT, at least from an applied perspective, is how fundamentally different it is from anything most people have encountered previously. Because many people are unfamiliar with the mathematical concepts that form the basis of IRT, it can be quite challenging to use and explain IRT to a nontechnical audience. CIRP, for example, faced many questions in the rollout of its constructs because the constructs' development, calculation, and meaning were foreign to most of the CIRP survey users. To ease the interpretation burden, CIRP eventually decided to provide both rescaled construct scores (to avoid negative values) and qualitative indicators of whether these scores were "high," "medium," or "low" (Sharkness et al., 2010).

Despite the challenge of implementation, IRT is clearly ideal for many applications in higher education. This chapter has described the basic tenets of IRT and has provided an example in which IRT was used by institutional researchers to assess and improve a student engagement scale. The creation of such scales is not the only profitable use of IRT in higher education, however. IRT can also help develop well-functioning outcomes assessment tests, can provide useful analytics about item bias, and can be used to easily link scores from populations not administered the same set of items. IRT has much potential to improve measurement in higher education; hopefully, we are just beginning to see what IRT has to offer.

Notes

1. For the purposes of this discussion, the terms *instrument*, *test*, and *survey* will be used interchangeably to refer to such measurement tools.

2. Measurement researchers have developed a variety of creative ways to get around the reliance on a particular set of items when using CTT, for example, by developing "parallel" forms of a test that are functionally equivalent but that contain different items (Allen & Yen, 1979/2000). However, all statistics calculated using CTT are fundamentally sample-dependent (Hambleton & Jones, 1993).

3. These are concepts covered on the depression inventory (for more information, see Beck, Ward, Mendelson, Mock, & Erbaugh, 1961); the definition of mild depression proposed is the author's own and is intended as a hypothetical example.

4. There are a variety of different IRT models for dichotomous data, some of which hold the steepness/slope constant across items. There are also models that introduce other parameters, such as those that take into account the guessing that may happen when a multiple-choice item is presented. Embretson and Reise (2000) describe these models and many others.

5. There are many other IRT models that can be used with polytomous data, both Likert and otherwise; see Embretson and Reise (2000) and Ostini and Nering (2006) for more details.

References

Allen, M. J., & Yen, W. M. (1979/2000). *Introduction to measurement theory*. Long Grove, IL: Waveland Press.

Astin, A. W. (1993). *What matters in college? Four critical years revisited*. San Francisco, CA: Jossey-Bass.

Baker, F. B. (2001). *The basics of item response theory* (2nd ed.). College Park, MD: ERIC Clearinghouse on Assessment and Evaluation.

Beck, A. T., Ward, C. H., Mendelson, M. M., Mock, J. J., & Erbaugh, J. J. (1961). An inventory for measuring depression. *Archives of General Psychiatry*, 4(6), 561–571. doi:10.1001/archpsyc.1961.01710120031004

Castro, S. M., Trentini, C., & Riboldi, J. (2010). Item response theory applied to the Beck Depression Inventory. *Revista Brasileira de Epidemiologia [Brazilian Journal of Epidemiology]*, 13(3), 487–501.

Chang, M. J., Han, J., Sàenz, V. B., & Cerna, O. (2008). The contradictory roles of institutional status in retaining underrepresented minorities in biomedical and behavioral science majors. *The Review of Higher Education*, 31(4), 433–464. doi:10.1353/rhe.0.0011

CIRP. (2009). *CIRP Construct Technical Report: Appendix—2009 Construct Parameters*. Los Angeles: Higher Education Research Institute, University of California. Retrieved from http://www.heri.ucla.edu/PDFs/constructs/Appendix2009.pdf

CIRP. (n.d.). *Frequently asked questions about constructs*. Retrieved from http://www.heri.ucla.edu/constructfaq.php

Embretson, S. E., & Reise, S. P. (2000). *Item response theory for psychologists*. Mawah, NJ: Lawrence Erlbaum Associates.

Hambleton, R. K., & Jones, R. W. (1993). Comparison of classical test theory and item response theory and their applications to test development. *Educational Measurement: Issues and Practice*, 12(3), 38–47. doi:10.1111/j.1745-3992.1993.tb00543.x

Harvey, R. J., & Hammer, A. L. (1999). Item response theory. *The Counseling Psychologist*, 27(3), 353–383. doi:10.1177/0011000099273004

Hurtado, S., Han, J., Sáenz, V. B., Espinosa, L. L., Cabrera, N. L., & Cerna, O. (2007). Predicting transition and adjustment to college: Biomedical and behavioral science aspirants' and minority students' first year of college. *Research in Higher Education*, 48(7), 841–887. doi:10.1007/s11162-007-9051-x

Kuh, G. D. (2001). *The national survey of student engagement: Conceptual framework and overview of psychometric properties*. Bloomington: Indiana University Center for Postsecondary Research and Planning. Retrieved from http://nsse.indiana.edu/2004_annual_report/pdf/2004_Conceptual_Framework.pdf

Ostini, R., & Nering, M. L. (2006). *Polytomous item response theory models*. Thousand Oaks, CA: Sage.

Reise, S. P., Ainsworth, A. T., & Haviland, M. G. (2005). Item response theory: Fundamentals, applications, and promise in psychological research. *Current Directions in Psychological Science*, 14(2), 95–101. doi:10.1111/j.0963-7214.2005.00342.x

Samejima, F. (1969). Estimation of latent ability using a response pattern of graded scores. *Psychometrika Monograph Supplement*, 34(4, Pt. 2).

Sharkness, J., & DeAngelo, L. (2011). Measuring student involvement: A comparison of classical test theory and item response theory in the construction of scales from student surveys. *Research in Higher Education, 52*(5), 480–507. doi:10.1007/s11162-010-9202-3

Sharkness, J., DeAngelo, L., & Pryor, J. H. (2010). *CIRP Construct Technical Report.* Los Angeles: Higher Education Research Institute, University of California. Retrieved from http://www.heri.ucla.edu/PDFs/constructs/technicalreport.pdf

Thorpe, G. L., & Favia, A. (2012). Data analysis using item response theory methodology: An introduction to selected programs and applications. *Psychology Faculty Scholarship, Paper 20.* Retrieved from http://digitalcommons.library.umaine.edu/psy_facpub/20

JESSICA SHARKNESS is the associate director of the Office of Institutional Research and Evaluation at Tufts University.

NEW DIRECTIONS FOR INSTITUTIONAL RESEARCH • DOI: 10.1002/ir

4

This chapter examines the relationship between student self-reported gains and college satisfaction, and it considers whether self-reported gains constitute a form of college satisfaction.

The Meaning and Interpretation of College Student Self-Reported Gains

Nicholas A. Bowman

Although many colleges and universities would like to conduct objective, longitudinal assessments of student learning outcomes, the financial resources and logistics required to collect such data are considerable. As a result, many institutions rely upon subjective measures as proxies for student growth. For instance, a survey might ask students to report their own learning and growth on a variety of outcomes, including critical thinking, subject matter knowledge, civic engagement, and understanding/appreciation of diversity. These self-reported gain items are used frequently on major college surveys, such as the National Survey of Student Engagement and previous versions of the Cooperative Institutional Research Program's College Senior Survey (these have not appeared since 2012). However, the meaning, interpretation, and usefulness of self-reported gains are highly contested (for recent discussions, see Bowman, 2013; Gonyea & Miller, 2011; Pike, 2011; Porter, 2013). Most of the recent attention and debate has focused on misinterpretations and misuses of these items, but far less attention has been paid to what these items may actually measure. The current study examined the relationship between college student self-reported gains and college satisfaction, and it explored the possibility that self-reported gains may be interpreted as students' satisfaction with their learning experience.

Literature Review

Researchers have often interpreted college students' self-reported gains as if they were indicators of actual learning and growth (Gonyea & Miller, 2011), but the preponderance of evidence suggests that this interpretation is not valid. According to several studies, the correlations between self-reported gains (e.g., in critical thinking) and longitudinal growth on valid measures

NEW DIRECTIONS FOR INSTITUTIONAL RESEARCH, no. 161 © 2014 Wiley Periodicals, Inc.
Published online in Wiley Online Library (wileyonlinelibrary.com) • DOI: 10.1002/ir.20067

of the same construct (e.g., a standardized critical thinking test) are either low or virtually zero (Bowman, 2010b; Bowman & Brandenberger, 2010; Gosen & Washbush, 1999; Hess & Smythe, 2001). Moreover, this correspondence is weak regardless of students' race/ethnicity, gender, academic preparation, parental education, and institutional type (Bowman, 2010a, 2011). Some scholars have argued that any disconnect between self-report and objective measures can be attributed (at least in part) to the fact that these two types of assessments capture different dimensions of the same construct (e.g., Dumont & Troelstrup, 1980; Pike, 1995). However, a recent meta-analysis (Sitzmann, Ely, Brown, & Bauer, 2010) found that the average correlation between self-assessments of knowledge and objective cognitive learning is moderate when attempting to report one's current knowledge ($r = .34$), but this relationship is nonexistent for examining gains in knowledge ($r = .00$). Thus, it seems that students have particular difficulty with estimating their own growth over time.

If self-reported gains do not accurately measure student growth, then what (if anything) do they measure? Some scholars believe that these items may serve as affective outcomes, broadly defined (Gonyea & Miller, 2011; Sitzmann et al., 2010). In their meta-analysis, Sitzmann et al. compared the extent to which self-assessments of knowledge were correlated not only with objective cognitive learning, but also with several affective outcomes: satisfaction with the instructional experience, motivation to apply the knowledge they gained, and self-efficacy for using that knowledge. Self-assessed knowledge is generally perceived to be a cognitive construct, so one might reasonably expect the correlation to be higher for cognitive learning than for the affective outcomes. Perhaps surprisingly, then, the average correlations with self-assessments of knowledge were significantly higher for satisfaction and motivation than for cognitive learning. Consistent with these results, Gonyea and Miller (2011) argue that college self-reported gain items—even those that ask about critical thinking and academic skills—should be viewed as affective outcomes. Within a large, multi-institutional sample, they showed that the perception of a supportive campus environment (which is an affective construct) was more strongly associated with several measures of college self-reported gains than was any other type of college experience. Finally, the correspondence between self-reported and longitudinal gains is consistently higher for noncognitive outcomes than for cognitive outcomes (Bowman, 2010a, 2010b, 2011), which lends further credence to this interpretation.

In an attempt to provide a more specific interpretation of self-reported gains, Bowman (2010b) suggested that they may largely—if not entirely—reflect students' satisfaction with their learning experience. That is, because students' perceived growth is virtually unrelated to their actual growth, students' self-reported gains may simply be an indicator of their satisfaction with their (perceived) learning and development. Porter (2013) recently discussed a psychological framework that would be consistent with this claim (also see Tourangeau, Rips, & Rasinski, 2000); specifically, he argued that college students likely use a belief-sampling approach when responding to self-reported gains. That is, instead of using the typical four-step cognitive process for responding to factual questions (e.g., college GPA), students instead recall a variety of beliefs, feelings, impressions, memories, and prior judgments (i.e., "considerations") to inform their survey responses. Indeed, the correlations among seemingly disparate domains of perceived growth (such as critical thinking and self-awareness) are generally high (Bowman, 2010b; Bowman & Brandenberger, 2010), which suggests that the considerations students use to generate responses could be similar across a broad array of items. Therefore, to the extent that similar considerations are elicited for different types of questions about the overall college experience, the correlation between college satisfaction and self-reported gain items should be high.

The available empirical evidence is consistent with this prediction: A few studies (most of which used a single-institution sample) have identified moderate to strong relationships between college satisfaction and self-reported gains (Bowman & Hill, 2011; Gonyea & Miller, 2011; Seifert & Asel, 2011). This research generally used single-item college satisfaction measures on which participants tend to respond favorably; in other words, most students reported being "satisfied" or "very satisfied," or (using a different scale) as having a "good" or "excellent" overall experience. Therefore, range restriction may be a significant problem, which means that prior studies may actually understate the correspondence between satisfaction and perceived growth.

Present Study

The present study systematically explores the relationship between college student self-reported gains and college satisfaction, and it examines the possibility that self-reported gains constitute a domain of college satisfaction. This project improved upon existing research in several ways. First, a large, multi-institutional data set was used, which helps enhance the generalizability of the findings. Second, to explore empirically whether the results differ among certain groups of students, subgroup analyses were conducted by gender, race/ethnicity, and family income. Third, multi-item measures of both college satisfaction and self-reported gains were used, which avoided earlier issues of range restriction and enabled these constructs to be assessed more adequately. Fourth, factor analysis and structural equation modeling (SEM) were used to examine the possibility that self-reported gains constitute a domain of college satisfaction; if this is true, then the "traditional" satisfaction items and the self-reported gain items should be adequately represented by a single latent factor.

Method

This study explored the meaning of self-reported gains within a racially diverse, multi-institutional sample.

Data Source and Participants.   The data source for this study is the National Longitudinal Survey of Freshmen (NLSF), which consists of undergraduates from 28 selective colleges and universities in the United States (for more information, see NLSF, 2013). In fall 1999, 3,924 first-year students agreed to participate in the study (86% response rate). Approximately equal numbers of Asian American/Pacific Islander, Black/African American, Hispanic/Latino, and White/Caucasian students were sampled. Follow-up surveys were then conducted via telephone in spring 2000, 2001, 2002, and 2003; students who transferred to a different institution or who dropped out of college were followed and retained in the sample to minimize selection bias. A total of 3,098 students participated in the final phone interview during senior year (79% retest response rate). The final sample included 814 Whites/Caucasians, 798 Blacks/African Americans, 765 Asian Americans/Pacific Islanders, and 721 Hispanics/Latinos.

Measures.   Six items measured aspects of college satisfaction in the senior year; three of these asked about satisfaction with the academic experience, and three other items inquired about satisfaction with one's college choice. Six additional items indicated students' perceived growth during college; three items asked about preparation for postcollege life, two others inquired about relating to people from other races, and a single item pertained to becoming a better person. These items are listed in Table 4.1 (for all items, 0 = totally disagree, to 10 = totally agree). Composite variables that measured overall college satisfaction and overall self-reported gains were created.

Several demographic variables were used to examine whether the correlations or internal reliabilities varied across demographic categories. Gender was measured with a dichotomous variable (0 = male, 1 = female), and race/ethnicity was classified into the four groups noted earlier. Family income was indicated via three groups (less than $25,000 per year, $25,000–$74,999, and $75,000 or more).

Analyses.   Principal component factor analyses were used to examine the extent to which the satisfaction and self-reported gain items reflect one or more constructs (for an overview of this technique, see Garson, 2013). Specifically, three factor analyses were conducted using (a) the six college satisfaction items, (b) the six self-reported gain items, and then (c) all 12 items. Internal reliabilities were computed using Cronbach's alpha, and the Pearson correlation between the overall college satisfaction measure and overall self-reported gains measure was examined. The internal reliabilities and correlation analyses were also conducted within each gender, racial/ethnic, and family income subgroup.

NEW DIRECTIONS FOR INSTITUTIONAL RESEARCH • DOI: 10.1002/ir

To determine whether college satisfaction and self-reported gains are best conceptualized as distinct constructs or as reflecting the same construct, SEM analyses examined covariance matrices of the data with the statistical software program EQS 6.1. SEM describes a family of techniques that can be used to examine not only the extent to which a set of items reflects one or more constructs (as factor analysis does), but also the extent to which the data are consistent with one or more statistical models (see Kline, 2011). The constructs in this study were indicated with latent variables; to maximize goodness of fit, the items in each scale were grouped into parcels, and these parcels were used to create the latent variables (Bandalos, 2002). Specifically, four parcels were created (two college satisfaction parcels and two self-reported gains parcels) by computing the average of three items. All parcels were then standardized with a mean of zero and a standard deviation of one for inclusion in the structural equation models. To ensure that the models were properly identified, the path from one of the parcels to each latent factor was set equal to one (Kline, 2011).

Two structural equation models were used to conduct confirmatory factor analyses. First, a two-factor solution was tested in which a latent college satisfaction factor consisted of the two college satisfaction parcels, a latent self-reported gains factor consisted of the two self-reported gain parcels, and a correlational path between the two latent factors was included. Next, a one-factor solution was tested in which all four parcels were modeled as components of a single latent factor representing satisfaction/gains. Because these two SEMs were nonhierarchical, it was not possible to test whether one model had significantly better fit than the other (Kline, 2011). However, the relative strength of the goodness-of-fit indices was examined. Goodness of fit was assessed with the normed fit index (NFI), nonnormed fit index (NNFI), confirmatory fit index (CFI), chi-square statistic (χ^2), and the ratio of chi-square to degrees of freedom (χ^2/df). Reasonable goodness of fit is indicated by an NFI, NNFI, and CFI greater than .95 (Bentler & Bonett, 1980; Hu & Bentler, 1999) and a χ^2/df ratio less than 2.0 or 3.0 (Bollen, 1989).

Results

The exploratory factor analyses strongly supported a one-factor solution for college satisfaction. The first factor explained 56.6% of the variance, all factor loadings on the single factor were at least .65, and the internal reliability of this construct was strong ($\alpha = .83$). Similarly, a one-factor solution for self-reported gains explained 52.1% of the variance, all loadings onto a single factor were at least .68, and the internal reliability was .81. When all 12 items were used in the same analysis, the results provided support for a single satisfaction/gains factor. Specifically, a one-factor solution explained 44.6% of the variance (with an eigenvalue of 5.35), whereas a second factor would only have explained an additional 12.6% of the

Table 4.1. Items, Factor Loadings, and Internal Reliabilities for College Student Self-Reported Gains and College Satisfaction

	Loading (alpha)		
Item	College Satisfaction	Self-Reported Gains	College Satisfaction/Gains
	(.83)	(.81)	(.88)
I am satisfied with the quality of instruction I received at college.		.812	.724
I would recommend [name of college] to a friend or relative as a place to attend college.		.801	.737
I am satisfied with the professors I had at college.		.795	.685
I am satisfied with the courses I took at college.		.746	.730
If I had it to do all over again, I would choose to attend [name of college].		.697	.647
I am likely to contribute to [name of college]'s future fundraising efforts.		.650	.606
My college experiences have prepared me for the future.	.807		.748
College has better prepared me to deal with the real world.	.758		.680
College has given me a sense of mastery of the subjects I studied.	.697		.712
My college experience has made me a better person.	.694		.667
My college experience has improved my relationships with other racial and ethnic groups.	.686		.514
My college experience has made me more tolerant of other racial and ethnic groups.	.680		.506

variance (with an eigenvalue of 1.52). All 12 items had loadings greater than .50 onto the single factor, and 10 of the items had loadings greater than .60. The internal reliability of this combined satisfaction/gains measure was high ($\alpha = .88$). All factor loadings and reliabilities are provided in Table 4.1. Moreover, according to Cohen's (1988) criterion, the correlation between the overall college satisfaction measure and overall self-reported gains measure was large ($r = .61$).

Subgroup analyses showed that the results were consistent across demographic groups. That is, the internal reliabilities for the satisfaction/gains construct were high regardless of gender ($\alpha = .87$ for both women and men), race/ethnicity ($\alpha = .89$ for Blacks, $\alpha = .88$ for Latinos, and $\alpha = .86$ for Asians and Whites), and family income ($\alpha = .88$ for low-income and middle-income students, and $\alpha = .87$ for high-income students). The

Figure 4.1. Structural Equation Model Conceptualizing College Satisfaction and Self-Reported Gains as Related (Yet Distinct) Constructs

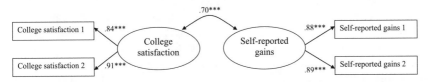

Note: To simplify presentation, errors and variances are not shown. ***$p < .001$.

correlations between overall college satisfaction and overall self-reported gains were also consistent by gender ($r = .61$ for women and $r = .60$ for men) and family income ($r = .63$ for low-income students, $r = .62$ for middle-income students, and $r = .60$ for high-income students). Although there was some variation in the correlations by race/ethnicity ($r = .65$ for Blacks, $r = .61$ for Latinos, $r = .59$ for Whites, and $r = .56$ for Asians), these relationships were invariably strong, and only one pair of correlations differed significantly from each other (Blacks versus Asians, $Z = 2.72$, $p < .01$).

The results for the two-factor model are shown in Figure 4.1. The data fit the model extremely well: NFI $= 1.000$, NNFI $= .999$, CFI $= 1.000$, $\chi^2(1) = 1.93, p = .16$. The bidirectional path of .70 means that the correlation between the latent constructs for college satisfaction and self-reported gains is .70 when adjusting for measurement error. Given this extremely high correspondence between constructs, it is reasonable to test whether the data might also fit well with a single-factor solution. Clearly, the data do not fit the single-construct model adequately, and the fit indices for this model were much poorer than for the two-factor model: NFI $= .809$, NNFI $= .429$, CFI $= .810$, $\chi^2(2) = 1076.90, p < .001, \chi^2/df = 538.45$.

Discussion

This study demonstrated that college satisfaction and self-reported gains are very closely related. The correlation between these constructs was quite strong, and a single factor that includes college satisfaction and self-reported gain items was highly reliable. Moreover, these correlations and internal reliabilities were consistent regardless of students' gender, race/ethnicity, and family income. These results suggest that the link between college satisfaction and perceived growth is stronger than in previous studies, which were generally not designed to test this relationship rigorously.

The results of the SEM analyses suggest that college satisfaction and self-reported gains are best conceptualized as two distinct—yet closely related—constructs. For the most part, students are likely attempting to provide accurate estimates of their own growth when asked to do so (Gonyea & Miller, 2011; Porter, 2013); as a result, their self-reported gains appear to diverge somewhat from direct measures of college satisfaction. It is quite possible that self-reported gain items could be tweaked slightly to become satisfaction items. For example, a survey could ask students how satisfied they are with their overall growth or with their learning and growth in specific domains. These items would then be a subset of college satisfaction by definition, and the correlation between this form of satisfaction and overall self-reported gains would likely be even higher than in the current study.

The present findings are consistent with the emerging view that self-reported gains constitute affective measures (Gonyea & Miller, 2011; Sitzmann et al., 2010) and that the considerations (i.e., memories, impressions, beliefs, and prior judgments) participants use to generate satisfaction and perceived growth responses may be quite similar. Further research is needed to explore issues of college students' survey responses. A more nuanced understanding of students' cognitive processes, along with the errors associated with survey responses, will help researchers and practitioners design questionnaires that may yield increasingly valid data.

Some limitations in this study should be noted. First, the sample includes only selective colleges and universities, so the results observed here may not generalize to less selective institutions. Second, only one of the self-reported gain items was explicitly related to cognitive or academic outcomes, so the overall self-reported gains construct may be less cognitive in nature than other composite measures of perceived growth. Third, many college student surveys contain more than six items that measure self-reported gains, so the relatively small number of items may also limit the scope of this global outcome.

Conclusion

In sum, college student self-reported gains are very closely related to—but not synonymous with—college satisfaction. Given the high correspondence between these constructs, the extent to which self-reported gains provide valuable information above and beyond college satisfaction and other student perceptions merits discussion. For instance, if students report being highly satisfied with their preparation for postcollege life and their classroom experiences, then is it useful to know students' self-reported gains in "practical competence"? In addition, if students perceive a positive campus climate for diversity and they engage in frequent, positive interactions across difference, then is it helpful to know the extent to which students think that they have gained in their appreciation of diversity? In general, institutional researchers, practitioners, and administrators benefit from having multiple forms of evidence about student experiences and outcomes. However, a broader conversation is needed about whether self-reported gains on programmatic, institutional, and national surveys should be replaced with other items that might provide more useful information regarding the experiences and outcomes of college students. Institutional researchers and scholars should develop, test, and advocate for alternative outcome measures that would help inform decision making on their campuses. The knowledge and experience that institutional research professionals possess could prove fruitful in shaping both local and national discussions regarding the improved assessment of college outcomes.

References

Bandalos, D. L. (2002). The effects of item parceling on goodness-of-fit and parameter estimate bias in structural equation modeling. *Structural Equation Modeling, 9,* 78–102.

Bentler, P. M., & Bonett, D. G. (1980). Significance tests and goodness of fit in the analysis of covariance structures. *Psychological Bulletin, 88,* 588–606.

Bollen, K. A. (1989). *Structural equation models with latent variables.* New York, NY: Wiley.

Bowman, N. A. (2010a). Assessing learning and development among diverse college students. In S. Herzog (Ed.), *New Directions for Institutional Research: No. 145. Diversity and educational benefits* (pp. 53–71). San Francisco, CA: Jossey-Bass.

Bowman, N. A. (2010b). Can 1st-year college students accurately report their learning and development? *American Educational Research Journal, 47,* 466–496.

Bowman, N. A. (2011). Validity of self-reported gains at diverse institutions. *Educational Researcher, 40*(1), 22–24.

Bowman, N. A. (2013). Understanding and addressing the challenges of assessing college student growth in student affairs. *Research & Practice in Assessment, 8*(Winter), 5–14.

Bowman, N. A., & Brandenberger, J. W. (2010). Quantitative assessment of service-learning outcomes: Is self-reported change an adequate proxy for longitudinal change? In J. Keshen, B. Holland, & B. Moely (Eds.), *Research for what? Making engaged scholarship matter* (Advances in Service-Learning Research, Vol. 10, pp. 25–43). Charlotte, NC: Information Age Publishing.

Bowman, N. A., & Hill, P. L. (2011). Measuring how college affects students: Social desirability and other potential biases in self-reported gains. In S. Herzog & N. A. Bowman (Eds.), *New Directions for Institutional Research: No. 150. Validity and limitations of college student self-report data* (pp. 73–85). San Francisco, CA: Jossey-Bass.

Cohen, J. (1988). *Statistical power analysis for the behavioral sciences* (2nd ed.). Mahwah, NJ: Lawrence Erlbaum.

Dumont, R. G., & Troelstrup, R. L. (1980). Exploring relationships between objective and subjective measures of instructional outcomes. *Research in Higher Education, 12,* 37–51.

Garson, G. D. (2013). *Factor analysis* (Statistical Associates Blue Book Series, No. 15). Asheboro, NC: Statistical Associates Publishing.

Gonyea, R. M., & Miller, A. (2011). Clearing the AIR about the use of self-reported gains in institutional research. In S. Herzog & N. A. Bowman (Eds.), *New Directions for Institutional Research: No. 150. Validity and limitations of college student self-report data* (pp. 99–111). San Francisco, CA: Jossey-Bass.

Gosen, J., & Washbush, J. (1999). Perceptions of learning in TE simulations. *Developments in Business Simulation & Experiential Learning, 26,* 170–175.

Hess, J. A., & Smythe, M. J. (2001). Is teacher immediacy actually related to student cognitive learning? *Communication Studies, 52,* 197–219.

Hu, L.-T., & Bentler, P. M. (1999). Cutoff criteria for fit indices in covariance structure analysis: Conventional criteria versus new alternatives. *Structural Equation Modeling*, 6, 1–55.

Kline, R. B. (2011). *Principles and practice of structural equation modeling* (3rd ed.). New York, NY: Guilford Press.

National Longitudinal Survey of Freshmen (NLSF). (2013). *National Longitudinal Survey of Freshmen*. Retrieved from http://nlsf.princeton.edu

Pike, G. R. (1995). The relationship between self reports of college experiences and achievement test scores. *Research in Higher Education, 36*, 1–21.

Pike, G. R. (2011). Using college students' self-reported learning outcomes in scholarly research. In S. Herzog & N. A. Bowman (Eds.), *New Directions for Institutional Research: No. 150. Validity and limitations of college student self-report data* (pp. 41–58). San Francisco, CA: Jossey-Bass.

Porter, S. R. (2013). Self-reported learning gains: A theory and test of college student survey response. *Research in Higher Education, 54*, 201–226.

Seifert, T. A., & Asel, A. M. (2011). The tie that binds: The role of self-reported high school gains in self-reported college gains. In S. Herzog & N. A. Bowman (Eds.), *New Directions for Institutional Research: No. 150. Validity and limitations of college student self-report data* (pp. 59–72). San Francisco, CA: Jossey-Bass.

Sitzmann, T., Ely, K., Brown, K. G., & Bauer, K. N. (2010). Self-assessment of knowledge: A cognitive learning or affective measure? *Academy of Management Learning & Education, 9*, 169–191.

Tourangeau, R., Rips, L., & Rasinski, K. (2000). *The psychology of survey response*. New York, NY: Cambridge University Press.

NICHOLAS A. BOWMAN *is an assistant professor of higher education and student affairs at Bowling Green State University.*

This chapter describes a study that compares two approaches (self-reported effort [SRE] and response time effort [RTE]) for identifying low-effort examinees in student learning outcomes assessment. Although both approaches equally discriminated from measures of ability (e.g., SAT scores), RTE was found to have a stronger relationship with test performance, identified more low-effort examinees, and led to higher mean performance upon filtering than the SRE approach.

Identifying Low-Effort Examinees on Student Learning Outcomes Assessment: A Comparison of Two Approaches

Joseph A. Rios, Ou Lydia Liu, Brent Bridgeman

As testing contexts that have low-stakes consequences for examinees have become more popular, interest in research on test-taking motivation has grown. According to the expectancy-value model, achievement motivation is influenced by both the individual's expectancies for success and the subjective value attached to success on the task (Eccles [Parsons] et al., 1983). That is, if an examinee does not place great value on the success of an assessment, the examinee's achievement motivation will be low. If this occurs, motivation acts as an extraneous factor unrelated to skill and ability construct(s) of interest (construct-irrelevant variance), and greatly impacts the validity of score-based inferences (Eklöf, 2006). However, it is important to note that although a test may be of minimal consequence to the examinee, the results may still be high stakes for other stakeholders such as teachers, schools, districts, or countries (American Educational Research Association, 2000). As a result, it is important to collect validity evidence for inferences made from testing contexts that present minimal consequences to examinees. As stated in the *Standards for Educational and Psychological Testing* (American Educational Research Association, American Psychological Association, & National Council on Measurement in Education, 1999): "When individual scores are not reported to test takers, it is important to determine whether the examinees took the test experience seriously" (p. 167).

New Directions for Institutional Research, no. 161 © 2014 Wiley Periodicals, Inc.
Published online in Wiley Online Library (wileyonlinelibrary.com) • DOI: 10.1002/ir.20068

Examinee motivation is of significant concern in three situations: (a) assessment programs that have serious potential consequences for institutions or groups (e.g., teachers), but little consequence for examinees; (b) pilot testing items that are not embedded in an operational context; and (c) measurement research conducted at colleges and universities in low-stakes settings (Wise & DeMars, 2006). In these situations, test results typically have practical applications, but the validity of such scores may be lacking when examinee motivation is low, as test performance may not be reflective of the underlying skills or abilities of the examinee. Such a relationship between motivation and test performance can have deleterious results. For example, Wise and DeMars (2005) found that across 12 empirical studies, motivated students scored on average 0.59 standard deviations higher than their unmotivated counterparts; however, it is unclear whether ability was controlled for before assigning participants to experimental conditions. Low levels of test-taking effort have also been found to impact the assessment of student growth, causing meaningful changes to evaluation ratings for a significant number of school personnel (Wise, Ma, Cronin, & Theaker, 2013). In addition, research conducted by Liu, Bridgeman, and Adler (2012), which examined data from a higher education student learning outcome assessment, provides evidence to suggest that the limited learning of college students suggested in the book *Academically Adrift* (Arum & Roksa, 2011) may be due to students' low motivation in taking low-stakes institutional assessments. These findings are particularly troubling and point to the need for institutional researchers to examine students' motivation when taking low-stakes assessments where the validity of test results may greatly impact institutional-level decision making.

Procedures for Obtaining a Proxy of Motivation

Three major approaches have been adopted to obtain a proxy of examinee motivation: (a) self-report measures, (b) response time information (RTI), and (c) person–fit statistics. However, the use of person–fit statistics has gained little traction as it was shown to have little relation to self-reported effort (SRE) and response time effort (RTE; Wise & DeMars, 2005). As a result, this approach was not considered further in this study.

Self-Report Measures.   Self-report measures are administered after the test to assess self-perceived levels of test-taking effort and/or importance. To date, two popular measures have been developed for the purpose of evaluating test-taking motivation. The first measure developed by Wolf and Smith (1995) consists of eight 5-point Likert-type items that measure a unidimensional test-taking motivation factor. This measure has been used or adapted in numerous research studies related to test-taking motivation (e.g., Lipnevich & Smith, 2009). However, a more recent self-report measure, the Student Opinion Scale (SOS; Sundre & Moore, 2002), extended the work of Wolf and Smith (1995) by incorporating Pintrich's (1988, 1989) theory of motivation to include two factors of motivation: importance and effort. From this perspective, motivation is based on:

> an individual's willingness to learn or to display learning...contingent on the individual's interest in the task or the perceived importance of the task, as well as his or her disposition to put forth the necessary work to complete the task. (Sundre & Moore, 2002, p. 8)

The SOS is composed of 10 items with both effort and importance being measured by five 5-point Likert items. Extensive validation work on over 15,000 students has been conducted on this measure. Numerous research studies have indicated internal consistency in reliability estimates ranging from 0.80 to 0.89 as well as consistently obtaining a correlated-trait, two-factor structure corresponding to importance and effort across multiple samples (see Sundre, 2007). The SOS is currently one of the most popular measures for assessing both examinee motivation and effort in low-stakes testing contexts, as it allows the user to separately report scores on the importance and effort constructs or combine their scores as a measure of examinee motivation (e.g., Liu et al., 2012).

Although self-report measures require very little resources to be administered, their use presents a number of limitations. For one, examinees who put forth little effort on the test may exaggerate their estimate of effort to be seen in a socially accepted manner. Alternatively, examinees who put great effort into the test may report reduced effort, which can be attributed to a belief of failure or lack of ability (Wise & DeMars, 2006). Therefore, it is difficult to ascertain how accurate examinees are in self-reporting motivation. An additional disadvantage is that self-report measures typically assess motivation at the test level instead of the item level. Though not addressed in this study, this aspect to the approach is potentially problematic as an examinee's motivation has been found to change throughout different phases of the test administration (Wise & Kong, 2005). Using this approach, one can only conclude overall whether an examinee is motivated or unmotivated, which results in completely filtering unmotivated examinees' data, thereby possibly ignoring valid responses that may have been provided. The RTI approach described next does have the benefit of being able to estimate valid item-level responses, though that is not a feature that is addressed in this study.

Response Time.   A strategy for obtaining a proxy of examinee effort is the use of RTI. This nonintrusive approach utilizes computer-based testing to identify engaged and disengaged examinees on the basis of the assumption that low-effort examinees will not take the necessary time to thoughtfully read through the item stem and all response options (i.e., they show a pattern of rapid guessing; Swerdzewski, Harmes, & Finney, 2011). The process of identifying low-effort examinees consists of first setting a threshold value that indicates rapid guessing. A number of methods have been proposed for this purpose, such as thresholds based on: (a) a common criterion for all examinees (Wise, Kingsbury, Thomason, & Kong, 2004), (b) item surface information (e.g., the number of characters in an item; Wise & Kong, 2005), (c) visual inspection of response time frequency distributions (Wise, 2006), (d) statistical estimation using a two-state mixture model (see Kong, Wise, & Bhola, 2007), (e) inspection of both response time and response accuracy distributions (see Lee & Jia, 2012), and (f) a percentage of the average item response time (Normative Threshold [NT] method; Wise & Ma, 2012). Once threshold values have been established for all items, an overall RTE index can be computed, which is the proportion of items on the test for which the examinee's response time was less than the established threshold values. The response time index for each examinee is then compared to a predetermined threshold value. Previous research has suggested that a response time index threshold value of 0.90 is reasonable (Swerdzewski et al., 2011; Wise & Kong, 2005), suggesting that a motivated examinee should display solution behavior for 90% or more of items. If the response time index is lower than the threshold value, the examinee's data are viewed as questionable and a candidate for filtering. Such an approach to filtering assumes that effort is unrelated to actual proficiency (Wise, 2009). To support this assumption, previous research has found response time index scores to be uncorrelated with independently obtained academic ability estimates where adequate examinee effort can be assumed (Wise & Ma, 2012). For example, Kong et al. (2007) found that response time index scores for 524 university undergraduates possessed nonsignificant ($p > .05$) correlations with SAT-Verbal and SAT-Quantitative scores for four different threshold procedures (common three second, surface feature, visual inspection of response time frequency histograms, and mixture models). Use of response time data for obtaining a proxy of examinee effort has been used in numerous research studies (e.g., Setzer, Wise, van den Heuvel, & Ling, 2013).

Comparison of Self-Report Effort and Response Time Effort. Given the relative recency of the interest on students' test-taking effort and the availability of response time data made possible by computer-based testing, there are only two studies comparing SRE and RTE in terms of identifying unmotivated examinees (Swerdzewski et al., 2011; Wise & Kong, 2005). Wise and Kong (2005) collected data from a low-stakes assessment by both recording response times and administering the SOS measure of effort. Examinees with raw scores ≤ 13 on the SOS effort subscale and/or rapid guessing on 10% or more of items were deemed unmotivated. These criteria were chosen on the basis of their stringency to filter examinees with low-effort profiles shown in previous research. Correlating response time with scores from the SOS measure produced a weak, positive correlation ($r = .25$, $p < .001$). In addition, the researchers looked to determine whether the response time and self-report measures were correlated with independently collected test scores in which examinee effort was likely to be high (i.e., SAT-Verbal and SAT-Quantitative scores). Low correlations with this outside measure are an indicator that the SOS is measuring effort in the low-stakes test session and not some general examinee trait. Results yielded nonsignificant correlations between RTE and SAT-Verbal ($r = .06$, $p > .01$) and SAT-Quantitative ($r = -.02, p > .01$) scores, whereas SRE was found to possess a statistically significant weak correlation with SAT-Verbal ($r = .14, p < .01$) and a nonsignificant correlation with SAT-Quantitative ($r = .01, p > .01$) scores. These results provided evidence that the methods were validly measuring specific test-taking effort and not serving as a proxy for a more general motivational profile or ability estimate. Furthermore, filtering low-effort examinees on the basis of RTE resulted in slightly higher mean scores when compared to filtering based on the self-report method for 460 examinees (Cohen's $d = 0.06$). These results led the authors to suggest that self-report and RTE may be measuring different aspects of examinee effort profiles.

Swerdzewski et al. (2011) went a step further in their analysis by examining agreement of low-effort examinee classification, comparing self-report and response time measures of effort on 2,965 university students. The same RTE criteria used by Wise and Kong (2005) were implemented in this study; however, Swerdzewski et al. chose a score of 15 or less on the SOS effort subscale as representing a low-effort profile. Results demonstrated a classification agreement of low-effort profiles ranging from 64.69% to 68.61% across six tests between RTE and SRE. Furthermore, the SOS measure tended to identify more examinees with low-effort profiles when compared to RTE scores. In addition, the authors found small increases in mean test scores when excluding students on the basis of the SOS and RTE filtering methods (effect sizes ranged from $d = 0.00$ to $d = 0.12$).

The previous studies shed light on two important points. First, although the empirical findings of the two studies obtained were relatively similar, Wise and Kong (2005) and Swerdzewski et al. (2011) differed in their support of RTE as a means of identifying low-effort examinees. Second, relatively large sample sizes were implemented in both studies that may not be comparable to the small sample size contexts observed in voluntary higher education student learning outcomes assessments. Therefore, as the two studies comparing the classification accuracy of low-effort examinees via self-report measures and RTI have reported mixed interpretations of findings with relatively large sample sizes (Swerdzewski et al., 2011; Wise & Kong, 2005), this study aims to provide further evidence of the comparability of these two methods in a small sample context. We address the following research questions:

1. Do SRE and RTE scores provide differential convergent and discriminant validity? That is, how strongly related are SRE and RTE scores to independent estimates of examinee ability? As filtering assumes that effort is unrelated to ability, how well do SRE and RTE scores

discriminate from measures of ability (cumulative GPA, SAT-Verbal, and SAT-Quantitative scores)?

2. Do SRE and RTE scores differ in how they classify examinees as showing low-effort profiles?

3. As we expect that the more effective filtering method should result in a higher mean score after the filtering, are there statistically significant and practically different score changes when comparing SRE and RTE methods?

Method

The following sections will describe the recruiting process, demographics of the sample, the measures used with accompanying validity evidence, and the analyses conducted to address the study objectives.

Participants.   The participants of this study consisted of 132 college seniors from five campuses of a state university system in the Midwest. Of these 132 participants, 80% identified themselves as White, 9% Black, 7% Latino/Hispanic, and 4% Asian American. All but one examinee were U.S. citizens, and most were English-dominant speaking (76%). Furthermore, the sample was comprised predominately of females (76%). Participants were recruited on a voluntary basis and were offered $25 to take the two-hour test.

Measures.   A computer-based version of the ETS Proficiency Profile (EPP), a 108-item college-level test assessing critical thinking, reading, writing, and mathematics, was administered to participants. Test administration was divided into two one-hour sessions resulting in a total of a two-hour testing window. The EPP has been shown to provide adequate average student-level ($\alpha = .78$) and institution-level ($\alpha = .90$) subscale reliabilities for all subscales. Furthermore, previous research supports the EPP's construct, content, predictive, and external validity (Belcheir, 2002; Hendel, 1991; Lakin, Elliott, & Liu, 2012; Liu, 2008; Liu et al., 2012; Marr, 1995). For example, the EPP has been found to be moderately to highly related to admission and placement test scores for a sample of 757 college freshmen (r ranged from .31 to .71, $p < .01$; Liu et al., 2012). Furthermore, on average, examinees with higher EPP scores have been found to obtain more course credits (Lakin et al., 2012; Marr, 1995). Upon completing the EPP, examinees were administered the SOS.

Analyses.   For the purposes of this study and to align with previous research (Swerdzewski et al., 2011; Wise & Kong, 2005), only the effort subscale (ranged from 5 to 25 score points) was used for comparability with RTE. Similar to Wise and Kong (2005), an SOS score ≤ 13 on the effort subscale was defined as representative of an examinee exerting little effort, and thus, requiring data filtering (removal). The evidence suggests that an SRE threshold of 13 is an accurate threshold for classification (Swerdzewski et al., 2011). This score corresponds to respondents reporting slightly less than moderate effort (on average 2.6 points on a 5-point response scale; Wise & Kong, 2005). For response times, effort was evaluated by first setting an item-level rapid-guessing threshold using a 10% Normative Threshold (NT10) method proposed by Wise and Ma (2012). In this method, a threshold is defined by taking 10% of the average item response time. For example, if, on average, examinees spent 50 seconds to answer a particular question, the NT10 would be 5 seconds. A maximum threshold value of 10 seconds was established as it may be difficult to credibly characterize a response of more than 10 seconds to be indicative of rapid guessing (Wise & Kong, 2005). Previous research has found the NT10 approach to be more effective than the three-second common threshold approach (Wise & Ma, 2012), which has been found to produce similar results to item surface feature, visual identification, and mixture model-based threshold methods (Kong et al., 2007). To determine the accuracy of the NT10 procedure, a proportion correct value (p value) was computed for all item responses identified as rapid guessing. If functioning correctly, the method would be expected to produce a p value near chance (25% for this test). In this application, the NT10 procedure was found to identify item responses that had a p value of .23, which aligns with previous findings that support the use of this method as a valid means of identifying random responding.

Upon determining rapid guessing for each item, RTE for each examinee was calculated as the ratio of the total number of items in which solution behavior occurred over the total number of items that the examinee answered. Similar to the two previous studies in this area, an RTE threshold of 0.90 was associated with unmotivated examinees, and thus was indicative of requiring data filtering. The reason that the RTE was applied at the test instead of item level was to ensure the comparability between RTE and SRE, as SRE was only available at the test level.

Results

Of the original 132 examinees, 30 were identified as unmotivated and filtered by the RTE approach, while 19 were filtered by the SRE method. Descriptive statistics on SAT scores, cumulative GPA, and EPP scaled score performance between motivated and unmotivated examinees across RTE and SRE methods are presented in Table 5.1. To ascertain whether examinees classified as low effort were of lower ability on independent estimates of their ability (i.e., GPA and SAT scores) than their motivated counterparts, Mann–Whitney U tests were conducted. The Mann–Whitney U test is a nonparametric procedure for independent measures that compares differences in totals of rank orderings between groups. It is akin to the independent t test; however, it relaxes distributional assumptions that may be difficult to meet with small sample sizes. Results of the Mann–Whitney U tests did not show a statistically significant performance difference between the low- and adequate-effort examinees identified by the SRE method

Table 5.1. Mean Ability and Test Performance for Motivated and Unmotivated Examinees

Variable	Self-Reported Effort		Response Time Effort	
	Motivated ($n = 113$)	Unmotivated ($n = 19$)	Motivated ($n = 102$)	Unmotivated ($n = 31$)
SAT-Verbal	512.44 (72.92)	496.15 (74.22)	510.00 (77.58)	511.30 (57.31)
SAT-Quantitative	523.54 (78.12)	522.31 (80.02)	517.20 (81.37)	536.09 (64.51)
Cumulative GPA	3.28 (0.48)	3.51 (0.29)	3.30 (0.49)	3.36 (0.42)
EPP scaled score	445.75 (23.19)	425.63 (19.04)	448.29 (23.38)	422.15 (11.09)

Note: Standard deviations are provided in parentheses.

on cumulative GPA ($U = 681.50$, $p = .09$), SAT-Verbal ($U = 513.50$, $p = .83$), or SAT-Quantitative scores ($U = 522.50$, $p = .91$). Comparable results between motivated and unmotivated examinees were found for the RTE approach on measures of SAT-Verbal ($U = 823.00$, $p = .74$), SAT-Quantitative ($U = 708.50$, $p = .20$), and cumulative GPA ($U = 1,566.50$, $p = .61$). As expected, unmotivated examinees possessed a lower mean scaled score on the EPP across both SRE ($U = 442.50$, $p < .01$) and RTE ($U = 532.00$, $p < .01$; see Table 5.1).

Convergent and Discriminant Validity of SRE and RTE Scores. Table 5.2 shows intercorrelations of the SRE, RTE, EPP, and external ability measures. The results can be interpreted with respect to convergent and discriminant validity analyses for SRE and RTE scores. Replicating previous findings, test-taking effort was strongly correlated with EPP performance (using Spearman rank-order correlations to account for small sample sizes). Both approaches demonstrated moderate-to-strong relationships with EPP scores; however, the observed correlation for RTE, $r_s = .67$, was slightly higher than that for SRE, $r_s = .58$. Interestingly, examinee effort (as represented by both SRE and RTE) had a stronger relationship with test performance than did measures of ability, such as cumulative GPA ($r_s = .06$), SAT-Verbal ($r_s = .40$), and SAT-Quantitative ($r_s = .32$) scores. In terms

Table 5.2. Spearman Rho Correlations Between Filtering Methods and External Variables

Measure	1	2	3	4	5	6
1. Test performance[a]	1.00					
2. Self-reported effort[b]	.58*	1.00				
3. Response time effort[c]	.67*	.61*	1.00			
4. SAT-Verbal[d]	.40*	.15	.09	1.00		
5. SAT-Quantitative[e]	.32*	.11	−.03	.56*	1.00	
6. Cumulative GPA[f]	.06	−.02	−.03	.17	.18	1.00

Notes: [a]$n = 132$; [b]$n = 113$; [c]$n = 102$; [d]$n = 98$; [e]$n = 98$; [f]$n = 132$; *$p < .05$.

NEW DIRECTIONS FOR INSTITUTIONAL RESEARCH • DOI: 10.1002/ir

of discriminant validity, both approaches were able to discriminate effort from examinee ability. More specifically, SRE possessed nonsignificant correlations with SAT-Verbal ($r_s = .15$, $p > .05$), SAT-Quantitative ($r_s = .11$, $p > .05$), and cumulative GPA ($r_s = -.02$, $p > .05$). The nonsignificant ($p > .05$) Spearman rank-order correlations of SAT-Verbal, SAT-Quantitative, and cumulative GPA with RTE were .09, $-.03$, and $-.03$, respectively.

Agreement Between SRE and RTE in Identifying Low-Effort Examinees. On the basis of the criteria set forth for both SRE and RTE, 107 of 129 (83%) examinees were classified identically as motivated/low effort across methods. Of the remaining 22 examinees, 18 (14%) were identified as low effort solely by the response time procedure and 4 (3%) were classified as low effort solely by SRE. As shown in Figure 5.1, SRE identified some examinees who did not display any rapid-guessing behavior (see the upper left panel), while RTE classified some examinees as unmotivated who self-reported high levels of effort (see the lower right panel). The relationship in classification between the two approaches was positive and moderate, $r_s(102) = .61$, $p < .001$.

Comparability of Mean Test Scores Using SRE and RTE Filtering Methods. The mean score differences between the unfiltered and filtered

Figure 5.1. Scatterplot of Classification Similarity Between the SRE and RTE

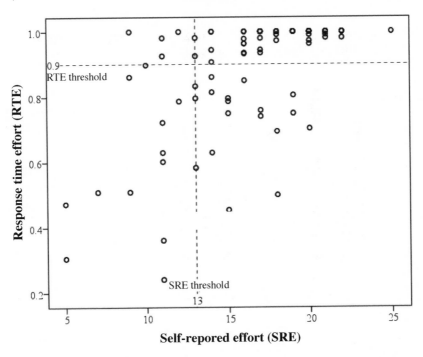

Table 5.3. Mean Test Scores on EPP for Unfiltered, RTE, and SOS Filtering Methods

Scale	Unfiltered ($n = 132$)		RTE ($n = 102$)		SRE ($n = 113$)	
	Mean	SD	Mean	SD	Mean	SD
Total	441.95	23.85	448.76	23.00	445.75	23.19
Reading	116.56	8.31	119.47	7.23	118.06	7.77
Writing	113.78	5.68	115.32	5.13	114.62	5.25
Math	112.97	7.27	114.22	7.48	113.90	7.24
Critical thinking	111.86	7.38	114.07	7.00	112.95	7.35

data sets were nonnegligible for some of the subscales, particularly when examining the difference between the unfiltered and RTE filtered data sets (Cohen's d ranged from 0.17 to -0.37). It is also of note that the variance was smaller for the RTE approach (for all but one subscale) than the unfiltered and SRE filtered approaches. Furthermore, the difference on the total and subscale scores between the RTE and SRE filtered data sets led to effect sizes that ranged from $d = 0.04$ to $d = 0.19$ (see Table 5.3 and Figure 5.2). Although these effect sizes are negligible to small, they are larger than those obtained in Wise and Kong (2005) and Swerdzewski et al. (2011). One possibility for this finding is that this study used a much smaller sample size

Figure 5.2. Effect Sizes of Mean Score Differences Between Filtering Methods

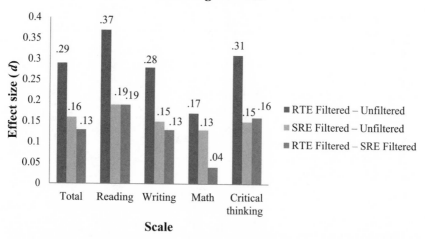

Note: RTE Filtered – Unfiltered = effect size from mean scores when comparing RTE filtered and unfiltered data sets; SRE Filtered – Unfiltered = effect size from mean scores when comparing SRE filtered and unfiltered data sets; RTE Filtered – SRE Filtered = effect size from mean scores when comparing RTE and SRE filtered data sets.

($n = 132$), which may have led to an increased impact of misclassifications on filtered mean scores between SRE and RTE. Such a sample size may be more prevalent in some contexts (e.g., higher education student learning outcomes) than what was found in the two previous studies.

Discussion

This study demonstrated that both SRE and RTE approaches identified examinee scores that were candidates for filtering because of low examinee effort. RTE was found to have a slightly stronger relationship with test performance and identified more examinees distinguished by their rapid response patterns, which led to small differences in mean scores between the two approaches. After filtering out examinees, the performance difference between filtered and unfiltered data sets was greater with RTE (d ranged from 0.17 to 0.37; Figure 5.2) than SRE (d ranged from 0.13 to 0.19). This suggests that RTE was more effective in removing low-score responders who lowered the overall test scores. As discussed in the literature review, SRE has a number of disadvantages that may have limited its accuracy in terms of identifying low-effort students. One of the disadvantages is that SRE is susceptible to response bias. The validity of SRE is threatened by examinees exaggerating their effort levels to be viewed in a socially acceptable way or reporting reduced effort (even though they put in great effort) due to a belief of failure or lack of ability (Antin & Shaw, 2012). In this study, 11.62% examinees reported high levels of effort through SRE, but their RTE data showed that they rapid-guessed on more than 10% of the items. In contrast, a small percentage of examinees (2%) did not employ rapid guessing on any items, but reported minimal effort through SRE.

Implications.   The findings from this study demonstrate the need for institutional researchers to evaluate examinee effort to ensure the validity of inferences made from low-stakes assessments. This assertion is supported by both the SRE and RTE approaches identifying 14% and 23% of total examinees as exerting low effort, respectively. The failure to filter examinees with low-effort profiles may significantly underestimate performance, as shown in this study. In the context of institutional research, such an underestimation could undermine the growth of student learning that has taken place as evaluated via a value-added model. This, in turn, could have negative implications for accountability, evaluation of institutional efficiency, and possibly, school-selection decisions by prospective students and parents (Liu, 2011). Although RTE was found to identify more examinees (with lower average scores) than SRE, SRE can also be a helpful tool in identifying low-effort examinees if RTE is not available (e.g., an institution administers a student learning outcomes assessment via paper–pencil format). However, given the necessity of the SRE procedure in administering an effort survey beyond that of the test of interest, RTE filtering may be the preferred method if response times are available.

Limitation and Future Research.   One limitation of this study is that the sample size was relatively small ($n = 132$), and therefore the findings may not generalize to examinees in other institutions or other types of tests. Future research should increase the sample size with examinees from other institutions to see if the findings still hold. We should also study college cohorts of other classes (e.g., only seniors were tested in this study), more varied demographics (e.g., majority of test takers were Whites in this study), different domains (i.e., some domains may require speeded responses), and use assessments of other types (e.g., locally developed assessment rather than standardized assessment). In addition, future research should examine different approaches to setting RTE thresholds. Currently, there have been a number of studies that have examined the comparability of RTE threshold approaches (see Kong et al., 2007; Wise & Ma, 2012); however, these studies have failed to examine these approaches under small sample size contexts. Further studying of threshold methods that strike a balance between filtering out valid data and failing to filter invalid data is also required.

Conclusion

This study confirmed that examinee effort is a potential source of construct-irrelevant variance that serves as a threat to the validity of score-based inferences in low-stakes testing contexts. Filtering data from low-effort examinees could significantly increase the mean scores and therefore impact the validity of inferences from assessment data. This study demonstrated that although both SRE and RTE approaches identified examinee scores that were candidates for filtering because of low examinee effort, RTE was found to have a slightly stronger relationship with test performance and identified more examinees distinguished by their rapid response patterns, which led to small differences in mean scores between the two approaches. These findings suggest that institutional researchers and scholars should consider applying data filtering using the RTE approach to inform score-based inferences. However, these findings also suggest that if practical constraints limit the application of computer-based test administration, which is required to obtain RTE scores, the use of SRE measures could also be an effective strategy for filtering invalid examinee data.

References

American Educational Research Association. (2000). Position statement of the American Educational Research Association concerning high-stakes testing in preK–12 education. *Educational Researcher*, 29(8), 24–25.

American Educational Research Association, American Psychological Association, & National Council on Measurement in Education. (1999). *Standards for educational and psychological testing*. Washington, DC: Author.

Antin, J., & Shaw, A. (2012, May). Social desirability bias and self-reports of motivation: A study of Amazon Mechanical Turk in the US and India. In *Proceedings of the SIGCHI Conference on Human Factors in Computing Systems* (pp. 2925–2934). Austin, TX: ACM.

Arum, R., & Roksa, J. (2011). *Academically adrift: Limited learning on college campuses.* Chicago, IL: University of Chicago Press.

Belcheir, M. J. (2002). *Academic profile results for selected nursing students* (Report No. 2002-05). Boise, ID: Boise State University.

Eccles (Parsons), J., Adler, T. F., Futterman, R., Goff, D. B., Kaczala, C. M., Meece, J. L., & Midgely, C. (1983). Expectancies, values, and academic behaviors. In J. T. Spence (Ed.), *Achievement and achievement motivation* (pp. 75–146). San Francisco, CA: W.H. Freeman.

Eklöf, H. (2006). Development and validation of scores from an instrument measuring student test taking motivation. *Educational and Psychological Measurement, 66,* 643–656.

Hendel, D. D. (1991). Evidence of convergent and discriminant validity in three measures of college outcomes. *Educational and Psychological Measurement, 51,* 351–358.

Kong, X. J., Wise, S. L., & Bhola, D. S. (2007). Setting the response time threshold parameter to differentiate solution behavior from rapid-guessing behavior. *Educational and Psychological Measurement, 67*(4), 606–619.

Lakin, J. M., Elliott, D. C., & Liu, O. L. (2012). Investigating ESL students' performance on outcomes assessments in higher education. *Educational and Psychological Measurement, 72*(5), 734–753.

Lee, Y.-H., & Jia, Y. (2012, April). *An investigation of response time in a NAEP computer-based assessment.* Paper presented at the Annual Conference of the American Educational Research Association, Vancouver, Canada.

Lipnevich, A. A., & Smith, J. K. (2009). Effects of differential feedback on students' examination performance. *Journal of Experimental Psychology, 15*(4), 319–333.

Liu, O. L. (2008). *Measuring learning outcomes in higher education using the Measure of Academic Proficiency and Progress (MAPPTM)* (ETS Research Report Series RR-08–047). Princeton, NJ: ETS.

Liu, O. L. (2011). Outcomes assessment in higher education: Challenges and future research in the context of voluntary system of accountability. *Educational Measurement: Issues and Practice, 30*(3), 2–9.

Liu, O. L., Bridgeman, B., & Adler, R. M. (2012). Measuring learning outcomes in higher education motivation matters. *Educational Researcher, 41*(9), 352–362.

Marr, D. (1995). *Validity of the academic profile.* Princeton, NJ: ETS.

Pintrich, P. R. (1988). A process-oriented view of student motivation and cognition. In J. S. Stark & R. Mets (Eds.), *New Directions for Institutional Research: No. 57. Improving teaching and learning through research* (pp. 55–70). San Francisco, CA: Jossey-Bass.

Pintrich, P. R. (1989). The dynamic interplay of student motivation and cognition in the college classroom. *Advances in Motivation and Achievement, 6,* 117–160.

Setzer, J. C., Wise, S. L., van den Heuvel, J. R., & Ling, G. (2013). An investigation of examinee test-taking effort on a large-scale assessment. *Applied Measurement in Education, 26*(1), 34–49.

Sundre, D. L. (2007). *The student opinion scale: A measure of examinee motivation.* Retrieved from James Madison University, Center for Assessment and Research Studies website: http://www.jmu.edu/assessment

Sundre, D. L., & Moore, D. L. (2002). The Student Opinion Scale: A measure of examinee motivation. *Assessment Update, 14*(1), 8–9.

Swerdzewski, P. J., Harmes, J. C., & Finney, S. J. (2011). Two approaches for identifying low-motivated students in a low-stakes assessment context. *Applied Measurement in Education, 24*(2), 162–188.

Wise, S. L. (2006). An investigation of the differential effort received by items on a low-stakes, computer-based test. *Applied Measurement in Education, 19*(2), 95–114.

Wise, S. L. (2009). Strategies for managing the problem of unmotivated examinees in low-stakes testing programs. *The Journal of General Education, 58*(3), 152–166.

Wise, S. L., & DeMars, C. E. (2005). Low examinee effort in low-stakes assessment: Problems and potential solutions. *Educational Assessment, 10*, 1–17.

Wise, S. L., & DeMars, C. E. (2006). An application of item response time: The effort moderated IRT model. *Journal of Educational Measurement, 43*, 19–38.

Wise, S. L., Kingsbury, G. G., Thomason, J., & Kong, X. (2004, April). *An investigation of motivation filtering in a statewide achievement testing program.* Paper presented at the Annual Meeting of the National Council on Measurement in Education, San Diego, CA.

Wise, S. L., & Kong, X. (2005). Response time effort: A new measure of examinee motivation in computer-based tests. *Applied Measurement in Education, 18*(2), 163–183.

Wise, S. L., & Ma, L. (2012, April). *Setting response time thresholds for a CAT item pool: The normative threshold method.* Paper presented at the Annual Conference of the National Council on Measurement in Education, Vancouver, Canada.

Wise, S. L., Ma, L., Cronin, J., & Theaker, R. A. (2013, April). *Student test-taking effort and the assessment of student growth in evaluating teacher effectiveness.* Paper presented at the Annual Conference of the American Educational Research Association, San Francisco, CA.

Wolf, L. F., & Smith, J. K. (1995). The consequence of consequence: Motivation, anxiety, and test performance. *Applied Measurement in Education, 8*, 227–242.

JOSEPH A. RIOS *is a graduate fellow at the Educational Testing Service.*

OU LYDIA LIU *is a managing senior research scientist at Educational Testing Service.*

BRENT BRIDGEMAN *is a distinguished presidential appointee at Educational Testing Service.*

6

The popularity of online student surveys has been associated with greater item nonresponse. This chapter presents research aimed at exploring what factors might help minimize item nonresponse, such as altering online survey page length and using progress indicators.

Survey Page Length and Progress Indicators: What Are Their Relationships to Item Nonresponse?

Shimon Sarraf, Malika Tukibayeva

Introduction

Online student surveys are central to the data collection efforts of many higher education scholars and institutional researchers. Unfortunately, their popularity has been associated with more frequent survey abandonment and item nonresponse, consequently raising concerns about data quality.

Discussions about college survey data quality often focus on response rates (Dey, 1997; Porter, 2004; Porter & Umbach, 2006), although item nonresponse is arguably very important as well, especially for institutional research staff who want to use a complete set of responses. A preference for a complete set of survey responses is not unreasonable since some surveys IR professionals administer are high stakes for campus policy development. With the administration of many student surveys on college campuses these days, students may become fatigued and less than willing to fully complete surveys, thus potentially biasing the results of survey questions that have fewer responses. Whether or not any particular question is biased due to item nonresponse is oftentimes difficult and unrealistic to determine, which partly explains the general desire for as little item nonresponse as possible. However, once a survey closes, institutional researchers must determine if any steps should be taken to address missing data points, either by imputation methods or deleting records that do not have responses to every question. Unfortunately, the simplest approach, deleting records with missing data, risks introducing error (Rässler & Riphahn, 2006), whereas implementing more reliable imputation methods may be more complex and time consuming than desired.

NEW DIRECTIONS FOR INSTITUTIONAL RESEARCH, no. 161 © 2014 Wiley Periodicals, Inc.
Published online in Wiley Online Library (wileyonlinelibrary.com) • DOI: 10.1002/ir.20069

This study explores what factors might help minimize occurrence of item nonresponse. Using experimental data from 14 colleges and universities that administered the National Survey of Student Engagement (NSSE), this study looks at how item nonresponse relates to survey page length and progress indicators (i.e., graphic, numerical, or textual information indicating extent of survey completion). Study results have direct implications for institutional researchers and scholars engaged in survey design suggesting that both survey format features can influence item nonresponse.

Literature Review

Online surveys are a primary data collection method for institutional researchers, higher education scholars, and policymakers. The advantages of online surveys in terms of cost and ease of production have led to their proliferation, but may have also contributed to decreased response rates (Tourangeau, Conrad, & Couper, 2013). In addition, the very nature of online surveys (as opposed to paper surveys or in-person interviews) may make it easier for respondents to abandon an online survey after answering some survey items, which results in higher survey breakoff rates (Tourangeau et al., 2013) and more item nonresponse (de Leeuw, Hox, & Huisman, 2003; Peytchev, 2009). If survey breakoff happens early enough in the survey-taking process where respondents do not answer enough questions, it can also result in a survey respondent being recorded as a nonrespondent (Tourangeau et al., 2013), thus lowering response rates. Under certain conditions, survey nonresponse and item nonresponse may compromise data quality and bias survey population estimates (Groves et al., 2009). Special statistical procedures to address missing data concerns may be employed, but researchers should recognize their limitations (de Leeuw et al., 2003). Consequently, whether or not one attempts to address missing data concerns, it is important to minimize breakoffs and item nonresponse by optimally formatting online instruments.

Although there are many reasons for survey breakoff, with some being beyond a researcher's control (Peytchev, 2009), certain online survey design features, such as progress indicators and the number of items included on a single survey page, can possibly be used in strategic ways to maximize the likelihood that a survey will be completed. Since the beginning of online surveys, survey scholars have recommended creating a sense of progress during the survey-taking process because, unlike paper survey respondents, online survey respondents do not always know how long it would take them to complete a survey (Dillman, Tortora, & Bowker, 1998). Although this perspective might be intuitive, recent inquiries into this topic have demonstrated mixed results: progress indicators, for example, have been shown to increase, decrease, or have no effect on breakoff behavior and item nonresponse rates. In an experimental survey administered to a sample of 2,520 first-year college students in Belgium, Heerwegh (2004) reported that a progress bar was related to decreased breakoff behavior, but this relationship was statistically insignificant. Another study found that the presence of progress bars only had a positive effect on breakoff rates when it was placed on a short survey, but no effect was seen with longer surveys (Yan, Conrad, Tourangeau, & Couper, 2010). Yet another study found that progress indicators do provide feedback to survey users as they complete a survey, but the information can lead to both higher survey completion rates and higher survey abandonment rates depending on users' perceptions of survey duration and difficulty completing the survey (Conrad, Couper, Tourangeau, & Peytchev, 2010).

These and other studies were examined in a meta-analysis conducted by Villar, Callegaro, and Yang (2013) examining progress indicators and breakoff behavior. The meta-analysis included 32 experiments and analyzed the results for three progress indicator types: constant, where steady progress is reflected throughout the survey; fast-to-slow, where progress is faster at the beginning and then slows; and slow-to-fast, where progress accelerates toward the end of the survey. Results indicated that subjects who experienced a constant progress indicator had slightly higher, but statistically insignificant, breakoff rates than those who did not see any progress indicator. In contrast, the other two progress indicator types showed statistically significant findings. Fast-to-slow progress indicators were associated with decreased breakoff, while slow-to-fast progress indicators showed increased breakoff. These findings support Conrad et al.'s (2010) conclusion that progress indicators can both help and hurt survey completion. When survey respondents initially perceive fast progress, survey completion is positively affected; conversely, when progress appears slow and completion is off in the distance, they communicate discouraging news and increase the likelihood of breakoff.

Another major question survey developers need to answer is how many survey items should be included on each online survey page (Tourangeau et al., 2013). The answer can range from one item to all items, but how might this decision affect data quality? Several studies have investigated this question. Based on responses from 21,000 undergraduates at the University of Michigan, Peytchev, Couper, McCabe, and Crawford (2006) found very few differences between scrolling and paging survey formats. The scrolling format placed all questions for each survey section on one page, requiring respondents to scroll with their internet browser to see every question. Alternatively, the paging format minimized the number of questions per page, ensuring respondents would see all questions without any need for scrolling. They found no difference in terms of response rates, the number of incomplete surveys, and breakoff rates, whereas differences in item nonresponse were negligible. Similarly, using a 40-item survey in the Netherlands, Toepoel, Das, and Van Soest (2009) found a very modest difference in item nonresponse between different survey versions that had either 1, 4, 10, or 40 items per page. In general, the study indicated that more items per page resulted in slightly more item nonresponse (e.g., subjects completed 0.1 more survey items with the 1-item per page version versus the 40-item per page version).

Study Purpose

Given the literature's mixed results when it comes to progress indicators and survey page length, survey developers should explore their influence on item nonresponse when formatting any particular survey instrument when possible. With this in mind, the NSSE, which is administered to first-year and senior students at several hundred institutions in the United States and Canada every year, experimented with several different survey formats. The investigation occurred in 2009 and 2011 when the standard online version of the NSSE instrument was 26 pages and did not use a progress indicator. The first 16 pages covered 85 core engagement survey items that asked respondents about their college experience. Most of these core items asked about the frequency of certain behaviors; others related to student perceptions of the campus environment as well as their self-reported learning and development. The remaining 11 pages of the survey included demographic-related questions (16 items), and one additional page allowed for respondents to comment about their college experience or the survey itself. Other pages included informed consent and general survey information. See nsse.iub.edu/html/survey_instruments.cfm for copies of the NSSE instrument by administration year.

NSSE conducted the experiment to learn more about the effects of two different progress indicator types and an increased number of survey items per page, thus requiring respondents to scroll down in order to view all survey items. According to Kaczmirek's (2009) classification, progress indicators are either graphic or textual. The experiment used each type by showing respondents either a progress indicator bar at the bottom of each survey page or a textual indicator that communicated the current page in relation to the total number of survey pages (e.g., "page 1 of 4"). See Figure 6.1 for the two different progress indicator formats this experiment used. NSSE staff eventually tested six revised survey versions and recruited institutions to administer them as part of their standard administration that primarily used the 26-page survey version without any progress indicator:

1. Four pages with no progress indicator;
2. Four pages with progress bar;
3. Four pages with page number (e.g., 1 of 4 pages);
4. Eight pages with no progress indicator;
5. Eight pages with progress bar; and
6. Eight pages with page number (e.g., 1 of 8 pages).

New Directions for Institutional Research • DOI: 10.1002/ir

Figure 6.1. NSSE Experimental Progress Indicator Types

Progress Bar

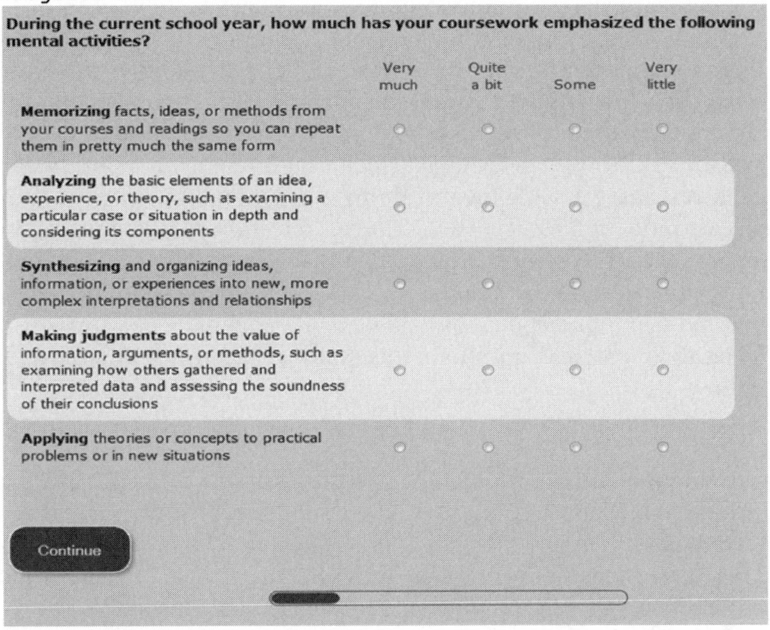

During the current school year, how much has your coursework emphasized the following mental activities?

	Very much	Quite a bit	Some	Very little
Memorizing facts, ideas, or methods from your courses and readings so you can repeat them in pretty much the same form	○	○	○	○
Analyzing the basic elements of an idea, experience, or theory, such as examining a particular case or situation in depth and considering its components	○	○	○	○
Synthesizing and organizing ideas, information, or experiences into new, more complex interpretations and relationships	○	○	○	○
Making judgments about the value of information, arguments, or methods, such as examining how others gathered and interpreted data and assessing the soundness of their conclusions	○	○	○	○
Applying theories or concepts to practical problems or in new situations	○	○	○	○

Continue

Page Number

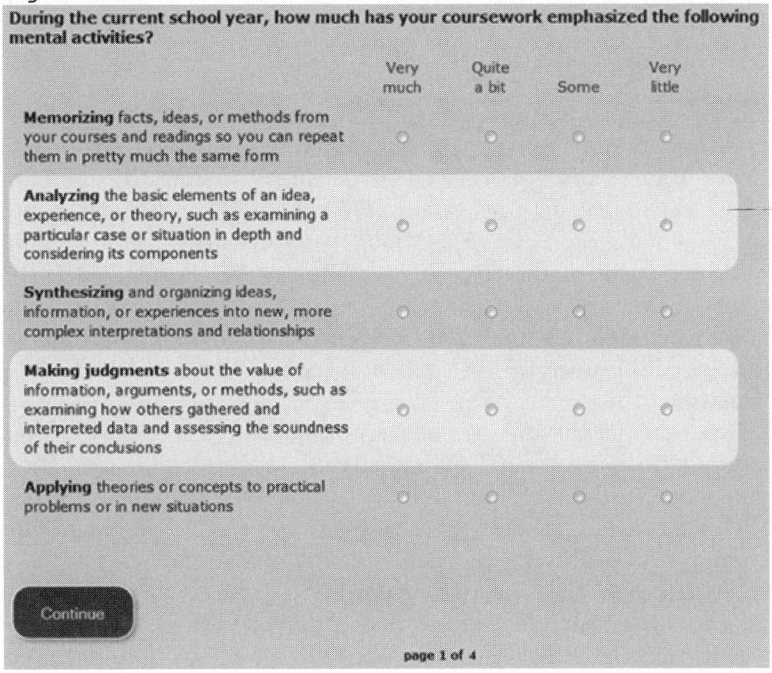

During the current school year, how much has your coursework emphasized the following mental activities?

	Very much	Quite a bit	Some	Very little
Memorizing facts, ideas, or methods from your courses and readings so you can repeat them in pretty much the same form	○	○	○	○
Analyzing the basic elements of an idea, experience, or theory, such as examining a particular case or situation in depth and considering its components	○	○	○	○
Synthesizing and organizing ideas, information, or experiences into new, more complex interpretations and relationships	○	○	○	○
Making judgments about the value of information, arguments, or methods, such as examining how others gathered and interpreted data and assessing the soundness of their conclusions	○	○	○	○
Applying theories or concepts to practical problems or in new situations	○	○	○	○

Continue

page 1 of 4

Although the vast majority of respondents taking part in the nonexperimental administration completed NSSE online, a small proportion of respondents at five institutions completed a 4-page paper version of NSSE as part of a "Web +" standard administration option that NSSE offered at the time to all participating institutions. Students at "Web +" institutions received their first three recruitment contact messages by e-mail. For the fourth contact, a random sample of nonrespondents received a paper version of the survey by standard mail (including a reminder about the online survey's availability) while the remaining nonrespondents received another e-mail recruitment message. Given the self-selection process involved with the paper survey respondent group rather than the random assignment used with the experimental conditions, any causal inferences regarding the paper survey and item nonresponse should be made with more caution.

The three research questions this study attempted to answer include the following:

1. Using the 26-page online NSSE instrument as a reference, does total item nonresponse count vary by the six different experimental survey versions?
2. Is one progress indicator type more effective than another at reducing item nonresponse, holding survey page length constant?
3. Does NSSE item nonresponse count vary by any student characteristics, holding all survey versions constant?

Methods

The sample for this study included 25,826 first-year and senior college students from 14 institutions who participated in either the 2009 and/or 2011 standard NSSE administration. In 2009, 20,035 students participated from 12 schools; in 2011, 5,791 students participated from 5 schools. Forty-five percent of the respondent sample were classified as first-year students at the time of survey completion (the other 55% were seniors), 91% were enrolled full-time, and 60% were female. The institutional sample included 11 doctoral research universities and 3 master's colleges/universities.

Experimental survey versions were administered at relatively large institutions with above average undergraduate student enrollments. NSSE recruited larger institutions intentionally because only these institutions had enough first-year and senior students to spare for the experiment without sacrificing data quality for the standard survey. With one exception, each 2009 school used all six experimental NSSE versions in addition to the standard 26-page version; schools that participated in 2011 used the two 4-page progress indicator versions along with the standard 26-page version with no progress indicator. The average item nonresponse and respondent

Table 6.1. Average Item Nonresponse Count by NSSE Survey Version

	Mean	n
Twenty-six pages	8.8	20,086
Four pages	9.9	570
Four pages with page numbers	8.1	1,108
Four pages with progress bars	7.6	1,172
Eight pages	11.2	639
Eight pages with page numbers	12.4	585
Eight pages with progress bars	11.0	1,534
Paper survey	1.5	132
Total	8.9	25,826

count for the six experimental survey versions, the standard survey version, and the standard paper version are included in Table 6.1.

Dependent Variable.   To test whether any experimental survey format related to item nonresponse, we calculated the total item nonresponse count using all NSSE survey items. Given 101 survey items, the outcome ranged from 0 to 100. Average item nonresponse for the entire sample was 8.8 with a median of 0. Sixty-one percent of respondents left no items unanswered, 18% had one, 5% had two, and 2% had three items unanswered. Remaining respondents distributed themselves fairly equally across other valid counts, with generally less than 1% falling into each of the remaining count values. For additional information about item nonresponse patterns by survey version, see Figure 6.2 for the percentage of respondents who left specific items unanswered along with indicators for the 8- and 4-page survey version page breaks.

Independent Variables.   Included among the independent variables were first-year class level (seniors as reference), full-time enrollment status (part-time students as reference), female gender (males as reference), and seven variables reflecting different survey versions, including the paper survey version, with the 26-page online NSSE survey used as reference. We coded each independent variable as either 1 or 0. Values of 1 indicated that a respondent used a specific survey version or was a member of a particular group when they completed the survey. Historically, first-year, part-time, and male students have responded to NSSE at lower rates (NSSE, n.d.), so we hypothesized they would also have greater item nonresponse counts than their peers and, therefore, serve as useful statistical controls. Descriptive statistics are provided in Table 6.2.

Statistical Models.   Given that the study's outcome variable is a count of item nonresponse, we investigated several different models designed for this type of data, including Poisson, negative binomial, and zero-inflated negative binomial models. Ordinary least-squares regression has often been used to model count data; however, the results can be inaccurate (Long & Freese, 2001). Based on statistical testing and theoretical

Figure 6.2. NSSE Item Nonresponse Percentages by Survey Version

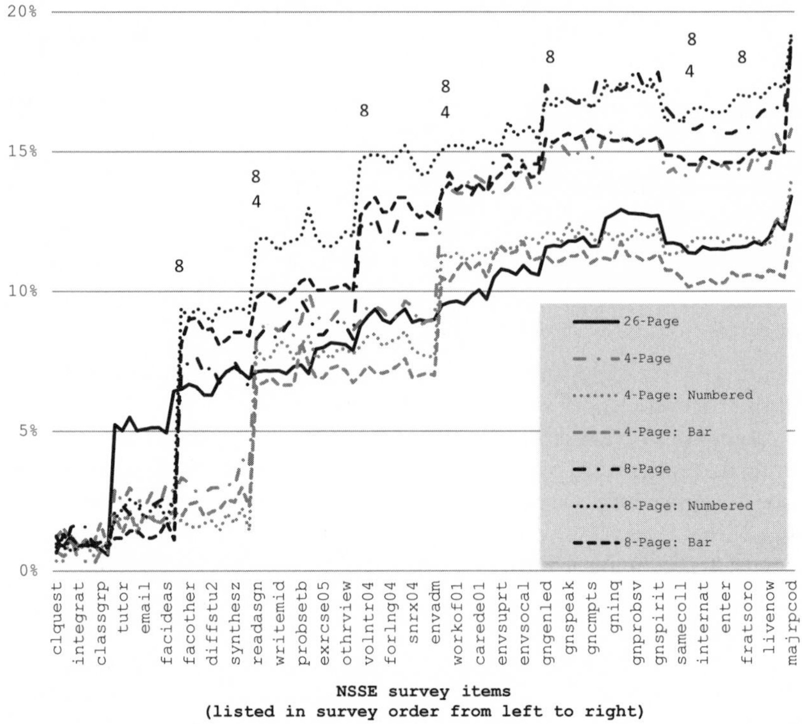

Note: "8" and "4" above lines indicate approximate location of page breaks for the 8-page and 4-page experimental survey versions.

reasons, we used negative binomial regression, which was ideally suited for an overdispersed dependent variable whose variance is substantially greater than its mean (Cameron & Trivedi, 1998). Using STATA 9.0 and the *SPost* package, we present model coefficients showing the change in the natural logarithm of the predicted count as well as the percentage change in expected count to simplify interpretation. In order to simplify even further, we also discuss change in terms of actual unanswered items using a hypothetical first-year, female, full-time student. We initially developed our model using the standard 26-page online survey as the reference group (referred to as Model 1) and later used 4-page and 8-page without progress indicator versions as reference groups (referred to as Models 2 and 3, respectively) to help evaluate progress indicator effectiveness.

In an earlier version of this study that also included institutions that did not administer any experimental survey versions, multi-level model results suggested that only 2% of the variation in survey item completion could be explained by institution-level characteristics (Tukibayeva & Sarraf, 2012). This study's sample using only experimental institutions

Table 6.2. Descriptive Statistics

Variables	Mean	Standard Deviation	Min	Max
Item nonresponse count	9.0	23.8	0	100
Survey versions				
Twenty-six pages	0.78	0.4	0	1
Four pages	0.02	0.1	0	1
Four pages with page numbers	0.04	0.2	0	1
Four pages with progress bars	0.05	0.2	0	1
Eight pages	0.02	0.2	0	1
Eight pages with page numbers	0.02	0.1	0	1
Eight pages with progress bars	0.06	0.2	0	1
Paper survey	0.01	0.1	0	1
Student characteristics				
First-year class level (reference: seniors)	0.45	0.5	0	1
Full-time status (reference: part-time students)	0.91	0.3	0	1
Female (reference: male students)	0.60	0.5	0	1

Note: $n = 25,826$.

shows that 0.8% of the variation in the outcome is explained at the institution level. Given these results, this study only used experimental institutions, forgoing a multi-level model and institution-level controls. Recognizing that student respondents would still be nested within the 14 institutions, we used the STATA *cluster* command to provide robust standard errors to provide more accurate statistical significance results.

Results

With regard to the first research question, we found that the three 8-page experimental survey formats had statistically significant greater item nonresponse counts than the 26-page version, holding all other independent variables constant (see Model 1 in Table 6.3). Responding to the 8-page version with no progress indicator increased the expected number of unanswered items by 38% ($p < .10$), or about four items for a first-time, female, full-time student, while the 8-page versions with page numbers and progress bars increased the expected item nonresponse count by 49% ($p < .01$) and 26% ($p < .01$), or five and three items, respectively. The three 4-page survey versions showed no statistically significant difference in item nonresponse compared to the 26-page survey, even though responding to the 4-page version increased the expected count of item nonresponse by almost 20% (n.s.). As these results suggest, using fewer survey pages (without progress indicators) generally increases the expected count of item nonresponse but not always in statistically significant ways. Finally, the paper survey format reduced the expected number of unanswered items by 82% ($p < .001$), or about eight items.

Table 6.3. Negative Binomial Regression of Survey Version and Student Characteristics on NSSE Item Nonresponse Count (Model 1)

	B	Standard Error	Significance	% Change in Expected Count
Survey versions				
Four pages	0.18	0.16		19.8
Four pages with page numbers	−0.01	0.09		−1.4
Four pages with progress bars	−0.10	0.12		−9.1
Eight pages	0.32	0.18	+	37.6
Eight pages with page numbers	0.40	0.14	**	49.1
Eight pages with progress bars	0.23	0.07	**	26.3
Standard paper survey	−1.72	0.14	***	−82.1
Reference group: 26-page survey				
Student characteristics				
First-year class level (reference: seniors)	0.30	0.05	***	35.1
Full-time enrollment status (reference: part-time students)	0.16	0.06	**	17.2
Female (reference: male students)	−0.08	0.03	*	−7.7

Notes: $^{+}p < .10$; $^{*}p < .05$; $^{**}p < .01$; $^{***}p < .001$.

In order to answer the second research question and better assess the impact of progress indicators, we reran our model using two different reference groups for survey version (see Model 2 in Table 6.4). Using the 4-page survey without progress indicator as the reference group, we found that using the 4-page survey with either page numbers or progress bars decreased the expected item nonresponse count by 18% (n.s.) and 24%,

Table 6.4. Relationship of Progress Indicator Type to NSSE Item Nonresponse Count

	Model 2		Model 3	
	% Change in Expected Count	Significance	% Change in Expected Count	Significance
Four pages	Reference group		−13.0	
Four pages with page numbers	−17.7		−28.4	+
Four pages with progress bars	−24.1	+	−34.0	*
Eight pages	14.9		Reference group	
Eight pages with page numbers	24.5		8.3	
Eight pages with progress bars	5.5		−8.2	

Notes: All results are based on negative binomial regression models that control for all survey versions, class level, full-time enrollment status, and gender.
$^{+}p < .10$; $^{*}p < .05$; $^{**}p < .01$; $^{***}p < .001$.

or about two items ($p < .10$), respectively, holding all other variables constant. Conducting a similar comparison for the three 8-page survey versions (see Model 3), we found that progress indicators of any type made no difference to the expected item nonresponse count. Although not presented in Table 6.4, we did test for differences between progress indicator types, holding survey page length constant. Results indicated no statistically significant differences.

As Table 6.3 shows, we found all three student characteristics to be statistically significant predictors for expected item nonresponse count. Being a first-year or full-time student (compared to senior and part-time students) increases the expected number of unanswered items by 35% ($p < .001$) and 17% ($p < .01$), respectively. In contrast, being a female student decreases the expected item nonresponse count by 8% ($p < .05$).

Limitations

This study has several limitations. First, not having a 26-page survey version with either progress indicator type prevented us from investigating whether, and to what extent, progress indicators might influence item completion for the 26-page survey version that did not require scrolling. Second, the study could have benefited from other survey page length formats in addition to the 4- and 8-page survey versions, since the gap between the 8-page and 26-page format is quite substantial. Having at least one other survey version with between 12 and 18 pages could have provided additional insights.

Other limitations relate to several potentially influential, uncontrolled factors in our statistical model. We do not know, for instance, how any campus incentives offered to students or general survey promotion efforts influence this study's results. It is possible to imagine, for example, that students receiving incentives may feel compelled to complete all survey questions. In addition, this study does not account for student academic background characteristics or academic performance, which can be positive factors in students' likelihood to participate and complete a survey (Dey, 1997; Porter & Whitcomb, 2005). We also do not know whether survey respondents paid attention to progress indicators. As shown in Figure 6.1, the format of progress indicators was not particularly conspicuous, especially in the case of the page number format. Conducting interviews with potential respondents and gathering their impressions about the placement of progress indicators may be worthwhile for better understanding these results.

Discussion

Our results suggest that dividing a relatively long survey into eight online survey pages would increase item nonresponse regardless of progress indicator usage. On the other hand, results indicate that survey items could be captured on four pages, requiring significantly more scrolling, with no substantial effect on the number of items completed. Reviewed separately, the six 4- and 8-page experimental versions might lead one to conclude that additional scrolling could either have no effect on item completion or be a detriment when compared to the 26-page version. This finding suggests a nonlinear, U-shaped relationship between survey page length or the amount of scrolling required and item nonresponse, at least with lengthier surveys such as NSSE. In some respects, this finding is not surprising given the mixed results found in the literature when it comes to survey breakoff and item nonresponse. Survey developers, however, should be careful not to generalize this study's results to surveys with many more or fewer survey items. When administering lengthier instruments such as NSSE, survey developers should consider optimizing perceptions of progress, thus minimizing item nonresponse, by testing different survey page lengths.

Although not the focus of this study, the paper version deserves particular mention again, given its large effect on item nonresponse. Results clearly show that the paper version has the least amount of item nonresponse compared to other formats. This may indicate that respondents are more likely to complete the survey when they can easily discern survey length. However, a more probable explanation is that students who are not interested in completing the entire survey (and decide to break off at some point) do not bother to return the survey in the mail, thus biasing item nonresponse counts. As explained earlier, these respondents chose to complete NSSE by pencil and paper, so notable differences in their behavior could very well be the result of uncontrolled respondent characteristics.

Our findings related to progress indicators mirror findings from Yan et al. (2010) where the presence of progress indicators with a long survey did not appear to affect survey completion. With one exception, Models 2 and 3 generally did not show statistically significant differences between the 4- and 8-page survey format without any progress indicator and the two progress indicator versions. However, coefficients suggest that progress indicators may still have some very modest influence on item nonresponse and that progress indicators interact with page length. The negative coefficients for both 4-page surveys with progress indicators in Model 2 compared to the reference group (4-page survey with no progress indicator) may suggest benefits of using progress indicators. By making similar comparisons between both 8-page formats with progress indicators and the 8-page format without progress indicator (reference group in Model 3), we see that progress bars appear to decrease item nonresponse, but page numbers do not. While these patterns were statistically insignificant for the most part, the relative consistency of results within the set of 4- and 8-page formats makes one think twice before concluding that progress indicators have no influence whatsoever on this particular outcome. Yan et al. (2010) concluded that one of their findings emphasized "the idea that progress indicators can help or can hurt, depending on whether they convey positive/encouraging or negative/discouraging information about movement through the task" (p. 145) of survey completion. Their view may also explain our progress indicator results whereby progress indicators in conjunction with very few long pages might convey a more encouraging feeling about moving through the NSSE survey. In sum, our results suggest progress indicators, especially a progress bar, to have a positive effect on survey completion behavior when significant scrolling is required as with the 4-page survey format. For this reason, we recommend evaluating page length and use of progress indicators together when designing surveys.

Another interesting finding from this study is that first-year students complete relatively fewer survey items than seniors. Although first-year students typically have lower response rates with NSSE, this result is still somewhat unexpected given that first-year students have not taken, presumably, as many surveys as seniors and would come to the NSSE survey generally less fatigued and therefore more likely to complete the survey. Of course, one might assume that seniors, who are close to graduation and have invested significant resources in their education, feel a greater need to give back to their institution by completing NSSE, an instrument that many campuses describe to students as being important to their efforts with bettering the institution. Given that better academic performance and preparation correlate with an increased likelihood for survey completion, as suggested by other studies, another possible explanation for this result may be that seniors leave fewer survey questions unanswered because they are academically stronger, on average, than first-year students once you take attrition into account.

With regard to the other two demographic variables included in our model, unsurprisingly, female students appear to answer more items than male students, which is consistent with their greater willingness to respond to NSSE in the first place. However, contrary to our expectations, part-time students appear to answer more survey items than full-time students, suggesting that, perhaps, they have more free time or are less distracted than full-time students, and thus likelier to complete the survey.

Based on these findings and our review of the literature, we offer the following conclusions for IR professionals as they think about formatting their online surveys. Let existing research studies about survey page length and progress indicators guide initial formatting decisions, but try, given sufficient resources and time, to pilot different survey formats in order to optimize item response. Our findings surprised us, namely the limited impact that progress indicators had and the existence of a curvilinear relationship between survey page length and item nonresponse, and expect that institutional researchers will also be surprised by what they discover with their own surveys that vary in length and content from the NSSE survey. Despite this study's modest support for the recommendation, we suggest using progress bars for surveys with many items spread across a minimal number of online survey pages (five or less) unless, of course, there is evidence particular to a certain instrument that suggests otherwise.

NEW DIRECTIONS FOR INSTITUTIONAL RESEARCH • DOI: 10.1002/ir

Institutional researchers might also consider asking themselves what is an acceptable level of item nonresponse before devoting significant time trying to minimize it. Given research that shows that population estimates are relatively accurate based on low response rates (Fosnacht, Sarraf, Howe, & Peck, 2013; Hutchison, Tollefson, & Wigington, 1987) and relatively few respondents (Fosnacht et al., 2013), a minimal amount of item nonresponse most likely introduces only a modicum of survey error into population estimates.

The findings of this study contribute to the growing body of literature focused on improving survey data quality. Given the widespread use of NSSE among higher education assessment professionals, more research needs to be done that explores different survey formats for minimizing item nonresponse.

References

Cameron, A. C., & Trivedi, P. K. (1998). *Regression analysis of count data*. Cambridge, UK: Cambridge University Press.

Conrad, F. G., Couper, M. P., Tourangeau, R., & Peytchev, A. (2010). The impact of progress indicators on task completion. *Interacting with Computers*, 22(5), 417–427.

de Leeuw, E. D., Hox, J., & Huisman, M. (2003). Prevention and treatment of item nonresponse. *Journal of Official Statistics*, 19(2), 153–176.

Dey, E. L. (1997). Working with low survey response rates: The efficacy of weighting adjustments. *Research in Higher Education*, 38(2), 215–227.

Dillman, D. A., Tortora, R. D., & Bowker, D. (1998). *Principles for constructing the web surveys* (Technical Report No. 98–50). Pullman: Washington State University Social and Economic Science Research Center.

Fosnacht, K., Sarraf, S., Howe, E., & Peck, L. (2013, May). *How important are high response rates for college surveys?* Paper presented at the Annual Forum of the Association for Institutional Research, Long Beach, CA.

Groves, R. M., Fowler, F. J., Couper, M. P., Lepkowski, J. M., Singer, E., & Tourangeau, R. (2009). *Survey methodology* (2nd ed.). New York, NY: Wiley.

Heerwegh, D. (2004, May). *Using progress indicators in web surveys*. Paper presented for the meeting of the American Association of Public Opinion Research, Phoenix, AZ.

Hutchison, J., Tollefson, N., & Wigington, H. (1987). Response bias in college freshmen's responses to mail surveys. *Research in Higher Education*, 26(1), 99–106.

Kaczmirek, L. (2009). *Human-survey interaction: Usability and nonresponse in online surveys*. Cologne, Germany: Halem Verlag.

Long, J. S., & Freese, J. (2001). *Regression models for categorical dependent variables using Stata*. College Station, TX: Stata Press.

National Survey of Student Engagement (NSSE). (n.d.). *An explanation of weighting in the NSSE Institutional Report*. Retrieved from http://nsse.iub.edu/html/weighting.cfm

Peytchev, A. (2009). Survey breakoff. *The Public Opinion Quarterly*, 73(1), 74–97.

Peytchev, A., Couper, M. P., McCabe, S. E., & Crawford, S. D. (2006). Web survey design: Paging versus scrolling. *The Public Opinion Quarterly*, 70(4), 596–607.

Porter, S. R. (2004). Raising response rates: What works? In S. R. Porter (Ed.), *New Directions for Institutional Research: No. 121. Overcoming survey research problems* (pp. 5–21). San Francisco, CA: Jossey-Bass.

Porter, S. R., & Umbach, P. D. (2006). Student survey response rates across institutions: Why do they vary? *Research in Higher Education*, 47(2), 229–247.

Porter, S. R., & Whitcomb, M. E. (2005). Non-response in student surveys: The role of demographics, engagement and personality. *Research in Higher Education, 46*(2), 127–152.

Rässler, S., & Riphahn, R. T. (2006). Survey item nonresponse and its treatment. *Allgemeines Statistisches Archiv, 90*(1), 217–232.

Toepoel, V., Das, M., & Van Soest, A. (2009). Design of web questionnaires: The effects of the number of items per screen. *Field Methods, 21*(2), 200–213.

Tourangeau, R., Conrad, F. G., & Couper, M. P. (2013). *The science of web surveys.* New York, NY: Oxford University Press.

Tukibayeva, M., & Sarraf, S. (2012, April). *The relationship between survey page length, progress indicators, and item completion rates.* Roundtable session presented at the Annual Meeting of the American Educational Research Association, Vancouver, Canada.

Villar, A., Callegaro, M., & Yang, Y. (2013). Where am I? A meta-analysis of experiments on the effects of progress indicators for web surveys. *Social Science Computer Review, 31*(6), 744–762.

Yan, T., Conrad, F. G., Tourangeau, R., & Couper, M. P. (2010). Should I stay or should I go: The effects of progress feedback, promised time duration, and length of questionnaire on completing web surveys. *International Journal of Public Opinion Research, 23*(2), 131–147.

Shimon Sarraf is NSSE's assistant director for Survey Operations and Project Services at Indiana University's Center for Postsecondary Research.

Malika Tukibayeva is a doctoral student at Indiana University Bloomington, and a former NSSE research project associate.

This chapter discusses an experimental study that shows that the order of items on a questionnaire and the response options for those items both affect the results of college student surveys.

Effects of Item Order and Response Options in College Student Surveys

Nicholas A. Bowman, Jonathon P. Schuldt

Given numerous pressures toward greater accountability and transparency in higher education, obtaining high-quality data about students' experiences and outcomes is more important than ever. A number of recent studies have examined issues related to college student surveys, including survey nonresponse (Adams & Umbach, 2013; Laguilles, Williams, & Saunders, 2011), survey completion (Barge & Gehlbach, 2012; Laguilles et al., 2011), socially desirable responding (Bowman & Hill, 2011; Gonyea & Miller, 2011), and satisficing (i.e., suboptimal cognitive processing that results in low-quality responses; Barge & Gehlbach, 2012; Chen, 2011). As a whole, these studies suggest that careful attention and inquiry is critical for drawing valid conclusions from college student surveys.

This study explores two issues that have received very limited attention in higher education. First, the order in which items are presented may play a role in shaping students' responses. For example, the Cooperative Institutional Research Program's College Senior Survey (CIRP CSS) asked students about their own learning and growth at the beginning of the questionnaire from 2010 to 2012, whereas these items were placed differently—toward the middle of the survey—in the preceding 17 years (see Higher Education Research Institute [HERI], 2014). The National Survey of Student Engagement (NSSE) asked about self-reported gains toward the end of the questionnaire from 2003 to 2013 (appearing before the demographics), whereas these were somewhat closer to the middle of the instrument in 2000–2002 (NSSE, 2014). To what extent might these item order differences within and across surveys affect student responses?

Second, the response options that are provided for a given item or set of items may also shape the results. The CIRP CSS and NSSE, along with many other surveys that are administered within and across institutions, ask about the number of hours per week in which students engage in various activities

New Directions for Institutional Research, no. 161 © 2014 Wiley Periodicals, Inc.
Published online in Wiley Online Library (wileyonlinelibrary.com) • DOI: 10.1002/ir.20070

(e.g., studying, working for pay, socializing). Both of these major national surveys provide eight response options; however, the maximum response on the CSS is "over 20" hours/week compared with "more than 30" for the NSSE. To what extent might these modest differences affect survey results?

Literature Review

A body of research in survey methodology and psychology demonstrates that seemingly trivial differences in questionnaire design can have a pronounced influence on the answers elicited (for reviews, see Schwarz, 1999; Tourangeau, Rips, & Rasinski, 2000). Survey respondents were once largely assumed to consider any given questionnaire item in near-perfect isolation from neighboring items and to be capable of providing fairly accurate reports concerning a range of personal behaviors. However, numerous research findings have challenged these assumptions. In a classic example, Schuman, Presser, and Ludwig (1981) hypothesized that self-reported opinions about a controversial political issue (i.e., abortion) may partly hinge on the nature of a preceding question. To test this hypothesis, the researchers varied the order of two questions that asked whether the respondents would support legal abortions in scenarios when a woman (1) "is married and does not want any more children" and (2) "there is a strong chance of serious defect in the baby." Results showed that a majority of participants (61%) responded "yes" to scenario 1 when that question came first; when scenario 2 came first, however, the proportion of "yes" responses to scenario 1 dropped to fewer than half (48%). In explaining this observation, Schuman and colleagues posited that the thoughts rendered cognitively accessible, or primed, by the more specific of the two scenarios (scenario 2) constrained opinions regarding the more general one (scenario 1) when that item was asked second. In other words, once thoughts of serious birth defects were brought to mind, respondents may have found it more difficult to endorse scenario 1.

This type of cognitive-accessibility explanation for item order effects is common in many studies since the 1980s that explore what are known as cognitive aspects of survey methods or "CASM" (see Schwarz, 2007; Strack, 1992). Over the past few decades, variable response patterns observed under different item orders have come to be seen less as mysterious, random, or haphazard, and more as systematic, predictable outcomes of the basic processes governing human cognition. An instructive example comes from the domain of surveys on subjective well-being, which sometimes ask respondents to provide an overall assessment of life satisfaction in addition to their satisfaction with specific domains of life (e.g., work, dating). An experiment by Strack, Martin, and Schwarz (1988) showed that the order of these questions mattered greatly for the results obtained: When respondents first reported on their overall life satisfaction (general) and then reported on their dating satisfaction (specific), the correlation between these variables was small and nonsignificant ($r = .16$). In contrast, a strong and significant correlation emerged when their order was reversed ($r = .55$)—a finding that, considered in isolation, might lead an observer to conclude that one's dating life matters enormously for one's overall happiness in life. On the contrary, Strack and colleagues posit that when specific questions precede more general ones, response correlations are inflated because the thoughts rendered accessible by the first question can readily inform the more general judgment.

Similar insights have been gleaned about the impact of response option format on the distribution of survey responses. Although many behavioral frequency surveys tacitly assume that respondents' behavioral histories are well defined and readily accessible in memory, this is not always the case. Whereas respondents may have little trouble accurately recalling how often they have broken a leg in the past two years, more frequent and mundane behaviors are represented more abstractly, opening the door for a variety of context effects when respondents are asked about them. For instance, Smyth, Dillman, and Christian (2007) asked college students to report the number of hours per day that they studied on a six-point scale. They randomly assigned students to respond to either a low-range scale (i.e., the largest category was "more than 2½ hours") or a high-range scale (i.e., the smallest category was "2½ hours or less"). Because instances of such common behaviors likely blend together in memory, the researchers expected responses to be swayed by the social norm implied by the given scale (i.e., low vs. high studying). Indeed, 70% of students reported studying 2.5 hours or less in the low-response option condition, whereas only 29% reported studying 2.5 hours or less in the high-range condition. Presumably, such results reflect the assumption among respondents that researchers have provided a meaningful and accurate distribution of response options, thereby freeing respondents to rely on their subjective sense of studying relative to others as opposed to a "recall and count" strategy for generating a response. It is now widely accepted that respondents engage in these sorts of social and communicative processes in attempting to make sense of the questions asked of them, as they would in any other conversational contexts (e.g., Schaeffer & Presser, 2003; Schwarz, 1996).

Present Study

Given the potential importance of order effects and response options on survey responses, this study examined these two issues within questionnaire designs that are similar to those in the NSSE and CIRP CSS, which are the two most prominent U.S. college experience surveys. By doing so, we hope to inform the practices of institutional researchers, practitioners, and scholars who study college students. While it is clear that a major shift in response options affects the results, would a fairly modest shift also have statistically and practically significant effects on a variety of college experiences? Similarly, although the order of specific versus general items seems to affect survey responses, would rearranging sets of commonly used questionnaire items alter the responses to these items?

Method

To examine possible effects of item order and response options in college student surveys, we conducted an experiment involving a diverse sample of undergraduates recruited from two U.S. universities. All participants were asked the same set of survey questions; only design features of the survey instrument (i.e., question order and response options) were varied depending on experimental condition.

Data Sources and Participants.   Participants were recruited from the psychology subject pools at two public universities: a regional commuter institution in the West and a selective flagship institution in the Midwest. A total of 439 undergraduates completed the survey (61% female, 38% Latino/Hispanic, 32% White/Caucasian, 11% Asian American/Pacific Islander, 9% multiracial/multiethnic, 7% Black/African American, and 3% other race/ethnicity). Students received partial course credit by participating in this online survey.

Measures and Procedure.   Across all experimental conditions, some indices were created from 2010 NSSE items (NSSE, 2009), which included academic engagement (20 items; 1 = never, to 4 = very often; α = .88), diversity interactions (2 items; 1 = never, to 4 = very often; α = .87), and self-reported gains (16 items; 1 = very little, to 4 = very much; α = .91). Other indices were created using 2009–2010 CIRP CSS items (HERI, 2009), which included sense of belonging (7 items; 1 = strongly disagree, to 4 = strongly agree; α = .84) and campus climate for diversity (3 items; reverse-coded so that 1 = strongly agree, to 4 = strongly disagree; α = .67).

Two randomized experiments were conducted simultaneously within the same sample, and participants could have been in any combination of experimental conditions. First, about half of participants were asked to provide self-reported gains before their college experiences and perceptions, and the other half were asked about self-reported gains after their college experiences and perceptions (demographics were assessed at the end of the questionnaire for all students). Second, participants were also randomly assigned to one of two response option conditions when reporting the hours per week spent engaging in 16 college behaviors, which were taken from the 2009–2010 CIRP CSS. One condition used the NSSE response options, which are about evenly distributed (0, 1–5, 6–10, 11–15, 16–20, 21–25, 26–30, more than 30); the other condition used the CSS response options, which are skewed toward smaller frequencies and with a lower maximum value (0, less than 1, 1–2, 3–5, 6–10, 11–15, 16–20, over 20). These responses were then recoded so that they could be compared across conditions. Since the CSS responses had a single category for "over 20," the NSSE responses of 21–25, 26–30, and more than 30 were combined into a corresponding single category. Similarly, the CSS categories of less than 1, 1–2, and 3–5 were combined for comparison with the NSSE category of 1–5. Although "less than 1" technically does not fit with any of the NSSE choices, we assumed that respondents to the NSSE items who engaged for less than an hour per week would not self-report that they never participated (i.e., by responding 0 hours/week). Thus, the six corresponding categories were 0, 1–5, 6–10, 11–15, 16–20, and over 20. Preliminary factor analyses showed that these 16 experience variables generally could not be combined into any coherent indices with one exception: the socializing, partying, and social network items could be combined into an overall socializing index ($\alpha = .64$).

Analyses. To examine the effect of the item order manipulation, t-tests were conducted for each of the indices (self-reported gains, sense of belonging, overall socializing, academic engagement, diversity interactions, and campus climate for diversity). Moreover, 16 chi-square analyses were conducted for the response option condition and each of the college experiences. Preliminary analyses showed that the assumption of an expected count of at least five for each cell was often violated. Therefore, the college experience variables were recoded by combining the three adjacent response options that generally had low frequencies so that there were four categories (0, 1–5, 6–20, over 20). The substantive empirical results for the four- and six-category variables were quite similar. Preliminary analyses also explored whether any experimental effects might be moderated either by the university that students attended or by each other (i.e., whether a certain combination of item order and response options might interact to yield unique results). No significant interactions were identified, so only the analyses of main effects are provided here.

Limitations. Some limitations should be noted. First, the sample only included two public universities. Although these institutions differ notably in terms of selectivity, region, and residential status, additional studies are needed to explore the generalizability of these results. Second, all participants completed the study online. While this survey mode has become quite popular for college student surveys, the results may differ for paper-and-pencil questionnaires. Third, only one order manipulation was conducted (i.e., moving self-reported gains to a different part of the questionnaire), so it is unclear whether and how other sequences would affect students' responses.

Results and Discussion

Participants who completed the self-reported gain items at the beginning of the questionnaire reported significantly higher academic engagement ($M = 2.68$ vs. 2.48, $t = 3.98$, $p < .001$, Cohen's $d = 0.38$), sense of belonging ($M = 2.99$ vs. 2.88, $t = 2.05$, $p = .04$, $d = 0.20$), and self-reported gains ($M = 2.93$ vs. 2.81, $t = 2.16$, $p = .03$, $d = 0.21$), as well as a marginally better campus climate for diversity ($M = 3.11$ vs. 3.01, $t = 1.80$, $p = .07$, $d = 0.17$) and more diversity interactions ($M = 2.87$ vs. 2.71, $t = 1.73$, $p = .08$, $d = 0.17$) than those who completed the self-reported gains toward the end of the questionnaire. No significant difference for overall socializing was observed ($M = 2.69$ vs. 2.61, $t = 0.83$, $p = .41$). These patterns suggest that students used their responses to previous items to inform their subsequent responses. Specifically, students tend to report that they make fairly substantial gains during college (e.g., NSSE, 2007), so those who completed self-reported gains first may be influenced to report levels of engagement and belonging that are consistent with those initial responses. On the other hand, many general college student surveys ask about a variety of experiences in which most students have not participated (e.g., student government, varsity athletics) or done so rarely (e.g., talking with faculty during office hours), which was also true within this study. Therefore, when students initially respond to college experience items, they may infer that they have not gained as much, since they previously reported having not engaged (or engaging very little) in many possible experiences. On the NSSE, self-reported gains are intentionally presented toward the end so that the earlier college experience and perception questions may inform students' responses to self-reported gains (Gonyea & Miller, 2011). This order likely improves responses for the college experience items that appear toward the beginning of the instrument (and therefore are not biased by any preceding items).

Table 7.1 contains the results for the chi-square analyses examining the relationship between the response option condition and the reported number of hours per week. Of the 16 analyses, 12 effects were significant ($ps < .05$) and two were marginally significant (student clubs/groups and partying, $ps < .10$); the effects were only nonsignificant for working on campus and working off campus ($ps > .66$). Because the hours that students work are systematically tracked—and are identical from week to week for many students—it is not surprising that changing the survey response options has no effect on these self-reports. The college experiences for which significant effects were observed ranged from those that might vary substantially across weeks and are difficult to keep track of (e.g., socializing, watching TV, and social networking) to those that would seem to be fairly consistent and predictable across weeks (e.g., attending class, praying, and commuting). The consistency of these effects across almost all experiences suggests the pervasive influence of response options for shaping self-reports.

To illustrate these effects in more detail, a typical example of the cross-tabulations (for time spent social networking) is shown in Table 7.2. As expected, a notably larger number of participants report spending 1–5 hours/week when this timeframe is represented by three response categories rather than just one. Similarly, a greater number of participants

Table 7.1. Results for Chi-Square Analyses of Survey Response Options and Self-Reported Time Spent Engaging in College Experiences

College Experience	Chi-Square	Significance
Attending classes/labs	7.96	*
Career planning (job searches, internships, etc.)	36.66	***
Commuting to class (driving, walking, etc.)	46.00	***
Exercising/sports	22.07	***
Online social networks (Facebook, MySpace, etc.)	23.46	***
Partying	7.48	+
Prayer/meditation	18.72	***
Socializing with friends	10.43	*
Student clubs/groups	6.78	+
Studying/homework	14.95	**
Talking with faculty during office hours	16.06	**
Talking with faculty outside of office hours	16.93	***
Volunteer work	13.23	**
Watching TV	11.66	**
Working (for pay) off campus	1.58	
Working (for pay) on campus	1.20	

Notes: Analyses each had 3 degrees of freedom. For all 16 experiences, more participants reported 1–5 hours/week in the low-maximum than the high-maximum condition, whereas more participants reported 6–20 hours/week in the high-maximum than the low-maximum condition. In addition, more participants reported over 20 hours/week in the high-maximum than the low-maximum condition for 14 of the experiences (both conditions had the same number of participants in this highest category for faculty interactions in office hours and out of class).
$^{+}p < .10$; $^{*}p < .05$; $^{**}p < .01$; $^{***}p < .001$.

report spending more than 20 hours/week when this timeframe is represented by three categories rather than one. The fact that there are a reasonably small number of students in this highest group is common across most experiences; with only a few exceptions (attending class, studying, socializing, and working off campus), the largest response option had the fewest students of any category. Interestingly, far more students reported spending 6–20 hours/week in the high-maximum condition (i.e., more than

Table 7.2. Cross-Tabulations for Survey Response Options and Self-Reported Time Spent Social Networking

| Experimental Condition | Value | Number of Hours per Week | | | | |
		0	1–5	6–20	Over 20	Total
Low-maximum condition	Count	16	139	51	11	217
(over 20 hours/week)	Column %	39.0	60.4	37.0	36.7	49.4
High-maximum condition	Count	25	91	87	19	222
(more than 30 hours/week)	Column %	61.0	39.6	63.0	63.3	50.6

New Directions for Institutional Research • DOI: 10.1002/ir

30) even though the categories were the same for this timeframe across the two conditions; this general pattern occurred for all 16 experiences. In the high-maximum condition, the categories for 6–10, 11–15, and 16–20 hours/week were among the middle out of the eight possible options (3rd, 4th, and 5th from the left, respectively), so these responses likely seemed more normative in this condition than in the low-maximum condition (in which they were 5th, 6th, and 7th, respectively).

Conclusion and Implications

This study showed that both item order and response options can affect college students' survey responses, which has important implications for institutional research and higher education scholarship. Many colleges and universities are interested in determining the extent of students' overall engagement, satisfaction, and intentions. Because the means and distributions for numerous constructs may vary depending upon the order in which items are administered and the response options that are provided, institutional decision makers might draw divergent conclusions depending upon seemingly trivial aspects of the questionnaire design. Moreover, in the controversial book *Academically Adrift* (Arum & Roksa, 2011), the authors argued that students generally spend too little time studying to achieve substantial learning gains. However, the conclusions about the average amount of time studying—and therefore whether that amount is "sufficient"—may depend considerably on the scale used to measure that learning. With the modest response option differences in this study, the proportion of students who reported spending 11 or more hours per week studying was 43% in the high-maximum condition, but only 31% in the low-maximum condition. Thus, these statistically significant effects are also practically meaningful.

The impact of response options broaches an important question: How should researchers and practitioners design questionnaires that yield the most accurate data? For most college experiences, the vast majority of students reported a fairly low number of hours per week (10 or fewer), which suggests that providing smaller categories would be more appropriate to differentiate among student responses and not to push students to report (overly) high values. However, many students do engage for extended periods of time in some experiences, such as attending class, studying/homework, socializing, and working for pay. Therefore, providing higher possible values for these experiences might be helpful and would be less likely to lead to "engagement inflation." For longer surveys, it would probably be best to include two sections with different response options for hours per week; these should appear far enough apart in the questionnaire so that participants are not confused by the shift in available choices.

Another approach would be to ask for open-ended responses so that students can enter the number of hours per week that they spend, which could subsequently be grouped into meaningful and appropriate categories. The benefit would be that students would not be affected by existing response categories, since the students would create their own value. However, there are at least two potential problems. First, for some experiences (e.g., social networking and watching TV), students may have so little idea of how long they spend that they would skip over this question entirely. These same students might be more willing to provide an educated guess when broad options are provided, which would lead to less missing data. Second, the potential for typographical errors could lead to substantially flawed results. In this situation, the researcher may have no idea whether the student intended to give this response or not; thus, s/he is faced with the unappealing possibilities of (a) removing a potentially correct and informative response, or (b) including a substantial, incorrect outlier that might bias the overall results.

As another practical question, in what order should survey items be presented to yield the most accurate responses? Dillman, Smyth, and Christian (2009) provide an excellent discussion of order effects; they group potential biases into cognitive-based effects (i.e., when early questions affect the processing of later questions) and normative-based effects (i.e., when early questions elicit a social norm that influences responses to later questions). The patterns in this study may have been influenced by both types of effects. That is, answering college experience questions first may have brought these experiences and related considerations in mind when responding to self-reported gains, which would be a cognitive-based priming effect. In addition, these participants may have also been seeking to align their level of engagement with their self-reported gains, which would be a normative-based consistency effect. Several of Dillman et al.'s specific guidelines for question order are also relevant for college student surveys: group related questions that cover similar topics, begin with questions that are likely to be salient to all participants, make the first question(s) interesting (which will also lead to higher completion rates), and ask questions about events in the order in which they occurred (when applicable). Satisfaction questions are particularly susceptible to order effects, so these should generally be asked early in the questionnaire. Moreover, overall satisfaction should be assessed first in a series of satisfaction questions, since the responses for overall satisfaction can be notably affected by reporting satisfaction in specific domains (e.g., Strack et al., 1988). It is also common practice to ask about demographics at the end of the survey; demographic responses are unlikely to be influenced by previous items, but they have the potential to shape participants' thinking regarding other types of items.

Future research should examine these issues in more detail. For instance, how might rearranging items about college satisfaction, student intentions (e.g., regarding retention/persistence), and campus climate affect student responses to these questions and others? Moreover, for both experimental conditions, this study examined changes in participants' responses to individual items and indices of those items. However, order manipulations can also lead to participants' providing answers that are either more similar or more different from one another across questions (Dillman et al., 2009); these dynamics among commonly used college student survey items should be explored. A strong understanding of the impact of questionnaire design is essential for supporting evidence-based decision making in higher education.

References

Adams, M. J. D., & Umbach, P. D. (2013). Nonresponse and online student evaluations of teaching: Understanding the influence of salience, fatigue, and academic environments. *Research in Higher Education, 53*, 576–591.

Arum, R., & Roksa, J. (2011). *Academically adrift: Limited learning on college campuses.* Chicago, IL: University of Chicago Press.

Barge, S., & Gehlbach, H. (2012). Using the theory of satisficing to evaluate the quality of survey data. *Research in Higher Education, 53*, 182–200.

Bowman, N. A., & Hill, P. L. (2011). Measuring how college affects students: Social desirability and other potential biases in self-reported gains. In S. Herzog & N. A. Bowman (Eds.), *New Directions for Institutional Research: No. 150. Validity and limitations of college student self-report data* (pp. 73–85). San Francisco, CA: Jossey-Bass.

Chen, P.-S. D. (2011). Finding quality responses: The problem of low-quality survey responses and its impact on accountability measures. *Research in Higher Education, 52*, 659–674.

Dillman, D. A., Smyth, J. D., & Christian, L. M. (2009). *Internet, mail, and mixed-mode surveys: The tailored design method* (3rd ed.). Hoboken, NJ: Wiley.

Gonyea, R. M., & Miller, A. (2011). Clearing the AIR about the use of self-reported gains in institutional research. In S. Herzog & N. A. Bowman (Eds.), *New Directions for Institutional Research: No. 150. Validity and limitations of college student self-report data* (pp. 99–111). San Francisco, CA: Jossey-Bass.

Higher Education Research Institute (HERI). (2009). *2009–2010 College Senior Survey.* Retrieved from http://www.heri.ucla.edu/researchers/instruments/FUS_CSS/2010CSS.PDF

Higher Education Research Institute (HERI). (2014). *Survey instruments, codebooks, and participation history.* Retrieved from http://www.heri.ucla.edu/researchersToolsCodebooks.php

Laguilles, J. S., Williams, E. A., & Saunders, D. B. (2011). Can lottery incentives boost web survey response rates? Findings from four experiments. *Research in Higher Education, 52*, 537–553.

National Survey of Student Engagement (NSSE). (2007). *Experiences that matter: Enhancing student learning and success—Annual Report 2007.* Retrieved from http://nsse.iub.edu/NSSE_2007_Annual_Report/index.cfm

National Survey of Student Engagement (NSSE). (2009). *National Survey of Student Engagement 2010.* Retrieved from http://nsse.iub.edu/pdf/US_paper_10.pdf

National Survey of Student Engagement (NSSE). (2014). *Survey instrument.* Retrieved from http://nsse.iub.edu/html/survey_instruments.cfm

Schaeffer, N. C., & Presser, S. (2003). The science of asking questions. *Annual Review of Sociology, 29*, 65–88.

Schuman, H., Presser, S., & Ludwig, J. (1981). Context effects on survey responses to questions about abortion. *Public Opinion Quarterly, 45*, 216–223.

Schwarz, N. (1996). *Cognition and communication: Judgmental biases, research methods and the logic of conversation.* Hillsdale, NJ: Erlbaum.

Schwarz, N. (1999). Self-reports: How the questions shape the answers. *American Psychologist, 54,* 93–105.

Schwarz, N. (2007). Cognitive aspects of survey methodology. *Applied Cognitive Psychology, 21,* 277–287.

Smyth, J. D., Dillman, D. A., & Christian, L. M. (2007). Context effects in web surveys: New issues and evidence. In A. Joinson, K. McKenna, T. Postmes, & U. Reips (Eds.), *The Oxford handbook of Internet psychology* (pp. 427–443). New York, NY: Oxford University Press.

Strack, F. (1992). "Order effects" in survey research: Activation and information functions of preceding questions. In N. Schwarz & S. Sudman (Eds.), *Context effects in social and psychological research* (pp. 23–34). New York, NY: Springer.

Strack, F., Martin, L. L., & Schwarz, N. (1988). Priming and communication: Social determinants of information use in judgments of life satisfaction. *European Journal of Social Psychology, 18,* 429–442.

Tourangeau, R., Rips, L. J., & Rasinski, K. (2000). *The psychology of survey response.* Cambridge, UK: Cambridge University Press.

NICHOLAS A. BOWMAN *is an assistant professor of higher education and student affairs at Bowling Green State University.*

JONATHON P. SCHULDT *is an assistant professor of communication at Cornell University.*

INDEX

Olitsky, N. H., 24
Operating characteristic curves (OCCs), 47–49
Ostini, R., 45, 47, 48, 57
Ott, M., 9

Page length, effect on item nonresponse. *See* Item nonresponse, survey page length and progress indicators and
Paper surveys, 84
Pascarella, E. T., 28
Pearl, J., 24
Peck, L., 96
Person–fit statistics, 70
Peytchev, A., 84, 85
Pike, G. R., 28, 59, 60
Pintrich, P. R., 70
Pohl, S., 24
Porter, S. R., 59, 60, 65, 83, 93
Presser, S., 100, 101
Progress indicators, effect on item nonresponse. *See* Item nonresponse, survey page length and progress indicators and
Propensity score (PS) analysis, 21; and counterfactual inference model, 22–24; data source and measures, 26–28; full matching method, 29; heuristic example, 26–37; literature review, 24–26; nearest neighbor matching method, 28–29; optimal matching method, 29; results, 29–37
Pryor, J. H., 56

Randomized controlled trials (RCTs), 3, 5–6
Rasinski, K., 61, 100
Rässler, S., 83
Regression discontinuity (RD) design, 4, 21; assumptions of, 9–12; bandwidth, choice of, 14–15; causal inferences, making of, 12–18; counterfactual framework, 4–6; crossovers in, 17; functional form, choice of, 15–16; fundamentals of, 6–12; fuzzy design, 9; regression discontinuity models, 13–14; running variable, 7–9; sensitivity analysis, 17–18; sharp designs, 8; treatment effect, estimation of, 16–17
Reisel, L., 27, 28

Reise, S. P., 41–49, 52, 56, 57
Response time effort (RTE), 72–74
Reynolds, C. L., 24, 36, 37
Riboldi, J., 46
Rios, J. A., 69–82
Riphahn, R. T., 83
Rips, L., 61
Rips, L. J., 100
Roksa, J., 70, 106
Rosenbaum, P. R., 22
Rubin, D. B., 22, 23, 26, 28, 29
Running variable, 7–9

Sáenz, V. B., 52
Samejima, F., 47, 52
Sarraf, S., 83–97
SAT-Quantitative score, 73
SAT-Verbal score, 73
Saunders, D. B., 99
Schaeffer, N. C., 101
Schmidt, W. H., 3, 5
Schneider, B., 3, 5
Schudde, L. T., 24, 37
Schuldt, J. P., 99–109
Schuman, H., 100
Schwarz, N., 100, 101
Seifert, T. A., 61
Sekhon, J. S., 28, 29
Self-assessed knowledge, 60
Self-reported effort (SRE), 72–74
Self-reported gains and college satisfaction, study on, 61; analyses, 62–63; data source and participants, 62; discussion, 65–66; literature review, 59–61; measures, 62; results, 63–65
Setzer, J. C., 72
Shadish, W. R., 3, 6, 17, 18, 21, 24, 25, 32, 33, 37
Sharkness, J., 41–58
Shavelson, R. J., 3, 5
Shaw, A., 79
Singer, E., 84
Sitzmann, T., 60, 66
Smith, J. A., 24
Smith, J. K., 70
Smythe, M. J., 60
Smyth, J. D., 101, 107
SOS. *See* Student opinion scale (SOS)
Spearman rank-order correlations, 76
Stable Unit Treatment Value Assumption, 23

IR 160   **Emerging Research and Practices on First-Year Students**
Ryan D. Padgett
As the demographic of college students continues to expand, higher
education researchers must thoroughly examine and reexamine what factors
contribute to students' lasting success. A myriad of research over the past few
decades have explored the impact of the first year of college on student
retention and success. With many state governing boards shifting budget
allocation initiatives to performance-based funding, institutional
administrators are taking a laser-focused approach to aligning retention and
success strategies to first-year student transition points.
This volume of *New Directions for Institutional Research* aims to enlighten the
discussion and highlight new directions for assessment and research practices
within the scope of the first-year experience. Administrators, faculty, and data
scientists provide a conceptual and analytical approach to investigating the
first-year experience for entry-level and seasoned practitioners alike. The
emerging research throughout this volume suggests that while many
first-year programs and services have significant benefits across a number of
success outcomes, these benefits may not be universal for all students. This
volume not only examines sophisticated empirical models but provides
critical assessment practices and implications. Additionally, responding to the
implication that the majority of research is on the four-year college, this
volume also examines the two-year setting, advancing the argument that
measuring the impact of the first year of college is just as critical at a
two-year institution.
ISBN: 978-1-1189-9363-7

IR 159   **Measuring Glass Ceiling Effects in Higher Education: Opportunities and
Challenges**
Jerlando F. L. Jackson, Elizabeth M. O'Callaghan and Raul A. Leon
An analysis of the United States workforce shows that women and people of
color represent an increasing share of employment in the economy in areas
previously dominated by White men, yet we still know very little in regard to
why these two groups continue to be underrepresented in senior-level
positions. The lack of empirical and practice-based research of glass ceiling
effects remains problematic.
This volume of *New Directions for Institutional Research* offers readers a
comprehensive means to understanding glass ceiling effects in higher
education. Each chapter approaches the glass ceiling from a different
perspective, providing compelling arguments that truly highlight the
importance and usefulness of collecting data on this topic. Institutional
decision makers will find valuable information to confront the challenge of
glass ceiling effects across different institutional environments. Likewise,
institutional researchers will find step-by-step protocols to collect and

analyze glass ceiling data as well as a variety of rich examples. Readers will not only find this sourcebook useful for institutional planning purposes, but it will also help them truly understand how the glass ceiling impacts women and people of color in higher education.
ISBN: 978-1-1189-5629-8

IR 158   **New Scholarship in Critical Quantitative Research: Part 1**
Frances K. Stage, Ryan S. Wells
Seven years ago, New Directions for Institutional Research published the volume *Using Quantitative Data To Answer Critical Questions*. In that volume, a group of quantitative researchers sought to differentiate their approaches to quantitative research from more traditional positivistic and postpositivistic approaches. The term *quantitative criticalists* described researchers who used quantitative methods to represent educational processes and outcomes to reveal inequities and to identify perpetuation of systematic inequities. The term also included researchers who questioned models, measures, and political processes, in order to ensure equity when describing educational experiences. These scholars resisted *traditional* quantitative research motivations that sought solely to confirm theory and explain processes. This volume provides an expanded conceptualization of those tasks and adds a third: to conduct culturally relevant research by studying institutions and people in context.
The chapters in this volume present work focused on underrepresented persons in a variety of levels of higher education. Each scholar has used critical quantitative approaches to examine access and/or success in the higher education arena. Their scholarship pushes the boundaries of what we know by questioning mainstream notions of higher education through the examination of policies, the reframing of theories and measures, and the reexamination of traditional questions for nontraditional populations. The work is divergent, but the commonality of the presentations lies in each scholar's critical approach to conventional quantitative scholarship. Their research highlights inequities and explores factors not typically included in conventional quantitative analysis.
ISBN: 978-1-1189-4747-0

IR 157   **Global Issues in Institutional Research**
Angel Calderon, Karen L. Webber
Globalization, demographic shifts, rapid technological transformation, and market-driven environments are changing the way higher education operates today. We know that human capital plays a critical role in the global economy, and postsecondary education is seen by officials in many countries as a key to economic development. Most developed countries have adopted policies for, or have considered, how to move toward greatly expanded higher education systems that can accommodate change. Globalized higher education produces an even greater need for the decision support function of institutional research; however, it needs to be debated in what form, shape, or orientation it should occur. All around the world, postsecondary institutions are facing competitive environments, declining resources, and changing societal needs. Institutions are affected by globalization, state and local government needs, economic restructuring, information technology, and student and staff mobility. Institutional researchers have a critical role to play in addressing these issues. In this volume, we have embedded the practice of IR as experienced globally. We brought together a discussion that is delivered

from multiple perspectives, but fundamentally one that draws from the collaborative efforts of practitioners across borders. By embedding notions of globalization that affect IR, we can engage readers in broad discussions on where we are coming from and where we are heading.
ISBN: 978-1-1187-1435-5

IR 156 **Benchmarking in Institutional Research**
Gary D. Levy, Nicolas A. Valcik
The term *benchmarking* is commonplace nowadays in institutional research and higher education. Less common, however, is a general understanding of what it really means and how it has been, and can be, used effectively. This volume of *New Directions for Institutional Research* begins by defining benchmarking as "a strategic and structured approach whereby an organization compares aspects of its processes and/or outcomes to those of another organization or set of organizations to identify opportunities for improvement."

Building on this definition, the chapters in this volume provide a brief history of the evolution and emergence of benchmarking in general and in higher education in particular. The authors apply benchmarking to enrollment management and student success, institutional effectiveness, and the potential economic impact of higher education institutions on their host communities. They look at the use of national external survey data in institutional benchmarking and selection of peer institutions, introduce multivariate statistical methodologies for guiding that selection, and consider a novel application of baseball sabermetric methods. The volume offers a solid starting point for those new to benchmarking in higher education and provides examples of current best practices and prospective new directions.
ISBN: 978-1-1186-0883-8

IR 155 **Refining the Focus on Faculty Diversity in Postsecondary Institutions**
Yonghong Jade Xu
Faculty diversity is gaining unprecedented emphasis in the mission of colleges and universities, and institutional researchers are being pushed for relevant data. In this volume, six chapters examine faculty diversity from a variety of perspectives. Together, they constitute a comprehensive outlook on the subject, highlighting factors including racial background, gender, citizenship, employment status, and academic discipline, and examining how growing diversity has affected the work experience and productivity of faculty and the learning outcomes of students. Special attention is given to international and nontenure-track faculty members, two groups that have experienced rapid growth in recent years. Chapter authors present empirical evidence to support the increasing importance of faculty diversity in institutional research, to show the need for actively tracking the changes in diversity over time, and to highlight the critical role of research methodology in all such work.
ISBN: 978-1-1185-2675-0

NEW DIRECTIONS FOR INSTITUTIONAL RESEARCH

ORDER FORM SUBSCRIPTION AND SINGLE ISSUES

DISCOUNTED BACK ISSUES:

Use this form to receive 20% off all back issues of *New Directions for Institutional Research*.
All single issues priced at **$23.20** (normally $29.00)

TITLE	ISSUE NO.	ISBN

Call 888-378-2537 or see mailing instructions below. When calling, mention the promotional code JBNND to receive your discount. For a complete list of issues, please visit www.josseybass.com/go/ndir

SUBSCRIPTIONS: (1 YEAR, 4 ISSUES)

☐ New Order ☐ Renewal

U.S.	☐ Individual: $89	☐ Institutional: $317
CANADA/MEXICO	☐ Individual: $89	☐ Institutional: $357
ALL OTHERS	☐ Individual: $113	☐ Institutional: $391

Call 888-378-2537 or see mailing and pricing instructions below.
Online subscriptions are available at www.onlinelibrary.wiley.com

ORDER TOTALS:

Issue / Subscription Amount: $ _____

Shipping Amount: $ _____
(for single issues only – subscription prices include shipping)

Total Amount: $ _____

SHIPPING CHARGES:

First Item	$6.00
Each Add'l Item	$2.00

(No sales tax for U.S. subscriptions. Canadian residents, add GST for subscription orders. Individual rate subscriptions must be paid by personal check or credit card. Individual rate subscriptions may not be resold as library copies.)

BILLING & SHIPPING INFORMATION:

☐ **PAYMENT ENCLOSED:** *(U.S. check or money order only. All payments must be in U.S. dollars.)*

☐ **CREDIT CARD:** ☐ VISA ☐ MC ☐ AMEX

Card number _____ Exp. Date _____

Card Holder Name _____ Card Issue # _____

Signature _____ Day Phone _____

☐ **BILL ME:** *(U.S. institutional orders only. Purchase order required.)*

Purchase order # _____
Federal Tax ID 13559302 • GST 89102-8052

Name _____

Address _____

Phone _____ E-mail _____

Copy or detach page and send to: **John Wiley & Sons, One Montgomery Street, Suite 1200, San Francisco, CA 94104-4594**

Order Form can also be faxed to: **888-481-2665**

PROMO JBNND